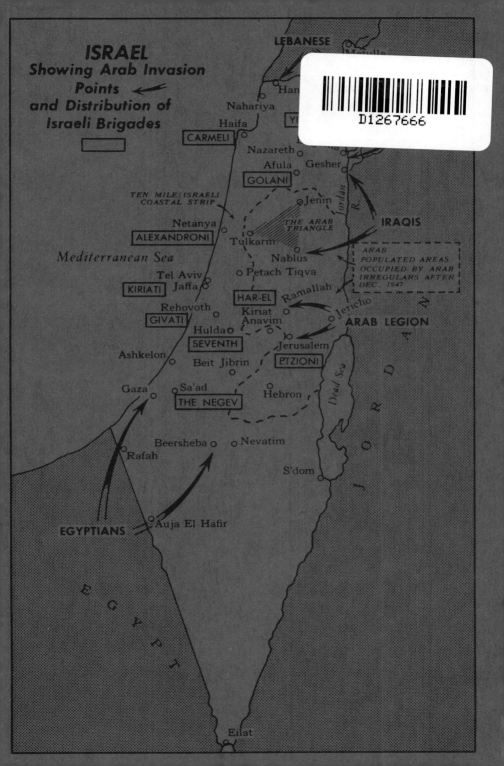

CAST A GIANT SHADOW

CAST A GIANT SHADOW

The story of Mickey Marcus,
a soldier for all humanity

by TED BERKMAN

The Jewish Publication Society
of America | Philadelphia
5728 | 1968

To My Parents
And All Others
For Whom Freedom Has
No Boundaries

PROLOGUE

High above the tranquil Hudson, where the grounds of the
United States Military Academy dip toward the shadowed
folds of Storm King Mountain, stands the West Point military cemetery. In this gallery of military immortals, one grave
is unique. It stands near the cemetery entrance, a few yards
from the shrub-lined path that winds west from the Old
Cadet Chapel. Here an American soldier was laid to rest on
a warm early summer's day in 1948. Among the mourners
were the governor of New York State, newly designated as
Republican candidate for the presidency; the wartime Secretary of the Treasury in the Cabinet of Franklin D. Roosevelt;
the chief officials of the City of New York; the underground
leader aboard the legendary refugee ship *Exodus*; and two
veteran field commanders who were soon to become the
Chiefs of Staff of the world's oldest and newest operating
democracies.

What chiefly sets this burial plot apart, however, is not the tributes paid that day, nor the cluster of battlefield and public glory that attaches to it. It is the only one, of all the three thousand-odd graves at West Point, that marks the resting place of a soldier killed fighting under a foreign flag.

The headstone is wedge-shaped and solid, as was the man who lies beneath it. The inscription it carries might justly have read: "Here lies a man who, after long and devoted service to his city and his country, felt democracy had unfinished business overseas. He carried his fight for human dignity to a struggling young republic far away, helping to shape a citizens' army. He carved out of naked mountainside the unseen road that saved the people of besieged Jerusalem, then fell at the city's gates, the first to hold the rank of General in the Army of Israel since biblical times."

The gravestone bears instead, in letters chiseled deep to withstand snow and wind and rain, the quiet legend: "Colonel David Marcus—A Soldier for All Humanity."

ONE

The pale young British sergeant, standing just inside his major's tent in central Palestine, brought up his hand to the tip of his beret in a crisp salute. "Jewish prisoners, sir."

"All right. Bring them in."

Three men, flanked by armed guards, filed from the blazing outside sunlight into the morning cool of the tent. The first two—an angular redhead and a slender blond youth with a scar running down his left cheek—wore the familiar dress of the Jewish colonizers in Palestine, khaki shirts and shorts purchased from British Army surplus. The third prisoner, stocky and older than the others, had no covering on his bronzed, burly chest. He walked with the loose, slightly rolling gait of the veteran athlete.

"Picked up the lot last night," the sergeant reported. "Parked in a jeep without lights, on the dirt road outside Ramleh."

The major was a tall Scot with a meditative eye. He slid into a chair behind a makeshift desk. "Any arms?"

"No, sir. But they had time to ditch them in the orange trees."

The major turned to the trio. "Why were your lights off?"

The redhead said something rapidly in Hebrew. The blond youth translated: "Battery trouble."

A skeptical nod. The British officer reached out a hand for the redhead's credentials. Silently a sheaf of papers was passed over, scrutinized. "Musician, eh?" commented the major. "I suppose it's the lost chord you were looking for, outside a strategic Arab town, in the middle of the night."

"We had been visiting friends in Beer Yaakov," came promptly from the young spokesman. "We were trying to find the main highway back to Tel-Aviv."

"Via a military survey of the terrain outside Ramleh?"

A noncommittal shrug. "I'm a farmer."

"The jeep had a bullet hole, sir," volunteered the sergeant. "In the left rear axle."

Again the swift, calm explanation. "From a hunting accident."

The major smiled wanly. There was no game in Palestine in that fading winter of 1947-48; only Arabs and Jews in an endless series of raids and reprisals, jockeying for positions in the decisive struggle that was certain to come when the British forces withdrew in May.

The previous November, the United Nations had voted for partition of Palestine into separate Arab and Jewish states. Arab political leaders, under the goading of the exiled former Grand Mufti of Jerusalem, had drowned their disappointment in a furious barrage of "crush-Zionism" slogans. Their words had caught fire. Already local Arab bands were shooting, dynamiting, and burning Jewish settlements and supply convoys wherever they could get away with it.

Privately, the major had a certain admiration for the way

the kibbutz dwellers refused to yield an inch under the in-
cessant attacks. But as long as Britain remained the manda-
tory power in Palestine, the major was a soldier under specific
orders: he was to strip the Jews of arms, and weed out the
leadership of their home-grown defense force, the Haganah.
This was no easy task, since the Haganah embraced virtually
the entire Jewish population. Men and women who in the
daytime were dentists and store clerks and schoolteachers
went underground at night, shouldering Sten guns and rifles
against Arab guerrilla centers.

The major thumbed through the blond prisoner's papers.
He glanced up. "Where'd you get that slash, Ben-Rov?"

"From a German bayonet. Jewish Brigade, His Majesty's
Forces."

The major was embarrassed. Many—altogether too many—
of these people had fought on the Allied side in World
War II, while Arab chieftains like King Farouk of Egypt
were flirting with the Axis.

"And now you're a farmer," the major mumbled. Then,
abruptly: "Let me see your hands."

Ben-Rov stepped forward.

The third member of the trio had been watching with silent
attentiveness, his quick black eyes darting from one to another of the players in the drama. Now, at the major's latest
command, he automatically directed his own gaze down-
ward. The muscles tightened across his barrel-thick chest.
Staring at him from the fourth finger of his left hand was a
large signet ring set with a ruby stone.

The ring measured perhaps three-quarters of an inch in
diameter. But inside that command tent in the British camp
of Sarafand it seemed suddenly enormous, and the red stone
glowing at its center was as arresting as a Times Square traffic
light; for the ring could identify its owner in a manner that
would jog the Colonial Office in London.

The chunky man scanned the room. The guards were all

concentrating on his colleague, now standing before the major, hands extended as if ready for a dive from a spring-board.

Very quietly, the man with the ring began twisting it around on his finger, so that if he were subjected to a similar examination, only the inside gold band would show on top.

Finally the major looked up. "No, no," he told Ben-Rov testily. "Palms up. I want to see how much work you've done in the fields."

"Palms up" was another story. As Ben-Rov obeyed, show-ing his work-toughened farmer's hands, the third man hastily restored the circle of metal on his finger to its original posi-tion.

And none too soon. "What about you?" the major was asking. "Do you speak English?"

The answer burst forth, clear and indignant. "Are you kid-din'? What's with this 'prisoner' routine? I'm a U.S.A. citi-zen, giving these jokers over here lessons on how to make with a foundry!" His high-pitched, banjo-string voice drew grins from the British guards. Nothing in his manner sug-gested he was the holder of three college degrees; a generous estimate would have given him a year or two in high school. He pulled a grimy wallet from his pocket and started extract-ing papers, passing them over rapidly to the major.

"Michael Stone," the Scotsman read aloud. "Steel mill foreman . . . employed by the Solel Beneh Foundation. . . ."

"Right, pal. Wanna see my hands?"

Without waiting for an answer, "Michael Stone" offered his broad, square-cut palms for inspection. They were cov-ered with a horny layer of tough callous.

"That don't come from handling tea cups, Mister!" Laugh-ter roared out of the chunky man in lusty waves, receding gradually into self-delighted chuckles that washed over the group.

The major's eyes traveled past the meaty forearms, up the

solid frame to the bulging, thickly corded neck. It was not hard to imagine this man melting and casting steel; in fact, it was a temptation to surmise that he was made of the stuff. Very possibly this was an innocent expedition. In any case, there was really nothing to hold these people on.

He handed back the American's papers and made a gesture of dismissal. "All right, Yank. Just—watch the company you keep."

The major turned curtly to the sergeant. "Let them go."

Driving off in their jeep, with the redhead at the wheel, the prisoners exchanged no words. Nor did they return, for the moment, to the orange grove where they had jettisoned a Sten gun and a revolver the night before on seeing the lights of an approaching British patrol car. Arms were precious, but this had been a narrow escape.

Late that afternoon, "Michael Stone" stood alone by an ancient sandy shore sunk deep below the cratered hills of Jerusalem. At his back, along the plain of Jericho, flowed the Jordan. Nearer by was the potash-working colony of Beit Ha'arava, one of the many isolated Jewish settlements already cut off from the heartland far to the west and reachable only by the kind of armed convoy that had just brought him here. In an hour he was to meet with leaders of the hard-pressed community and review their plans for its defense.

But meanwhile, he had a decision to make. He tugged reluctantly at the ruby-stoned band encircling his fourth finger.

This ring had traveled some 115,000 miles with him, through scores of countries spread over five continents. It had glistened on the beach of Honolulu; rested on polished conference tables at New York's City Hall and the White House, at Quebec and Yalta and Potsdam. And it had pressed against the night-chilled barrel of an automatic in Normandy.

Yet, if it were found on his person here the consequences

might be grim. About his own safety he had no illusions. Only the day before, he had written to a friend in America: "They play for keeps over here. If the British catch a Jew bearing arms in Arab territory, they take away his weapons and turn him over to the Arabs. Then, if you're lucky, you get your throat cut quickly."

What concerned him more was the secret mission in which he was engaged; this must not be jeopardized. The wise thing to do was to leave the incriminating ring behind him here, buried at the bottom of the Dead Sea.

But this was a man in whom logic sometimes had to make peace with sentiment. Security requirements could be adequately met, after all, behind a locked hotel safe in Tel-Aviv.

So Colonel David "Mickey" Marcus—athlete, government lawyer, and crusading city official; trainer of the Pacific's jungle-fighting Rangers, Pentagon planner, volunteer para-trooper in Normandy—slipped his college ring into his pocket. It was the first time it had been off his hand since his graduation from the U. S. Military Academy in 1924.

"Hi, Boss!"

Two days later David Ben-Gurion, future Prime Minister of Israel, looked up from his desk in Tel-Aviv at this un-conventional but already familiar greeting.

"Mickey! Come in!"

Mickey Marcus breezed through the door and flipped a thin leather brief case onto a chair. "Beautiful city you've got here." In street clothes—a coffee-colored sports jacket and brown flannels—he looked somewhat less formidable, although still charged with energy. His voice was high-pitched, as before, but now warm and easy.

"Been up since six-thirty," Mickey went on. "Had a swim, sun bath, little workout on the bars. You know, the first morning I woke up here, I thought I was in Miami

Beach. Then I got a load of those sidewalk cafes—and the pretty girls—and I decided it was Paris. Paris with date palms!"

Mickey broke into a laugh. It started as a soft, almost purring sound in the back of his throat, then erupted into a jovial, all-embracing roar of delight. One thing about his performance as "Michael Stone" had been not at all false: his booming laugh. It was virtually Mickey's trademark.

The stubby, white-haired Ben-Gurion, for all his preoccupation with the urgencies of politics, found himself giving an answering smile in response to the sheer good fellowship flowing from the American.

But the underground Chief of Government had other things on his mind. "Well, Mickey, you've had your look around. What do you think?"

Mickey's genial, oval-smooth face, almost cherubic until a second look underlined the taut furrows running from cheekbone to temple, darkened into a frown. "You want it straight, don't you, Boss?"

"Of course."

"All right: we're in trouble."

"That's what I suspected. How bad?"

"This bad . . ." Mickey chose his words carefully. "If the Arabs had a decent campaign plan—and they could attack in force tomorrow—collectively they have the military potential to take Tel-Aviv in ten days."

David Ben-Gurion slammed shut the huge Bible open on his desk.

"Just matching strength against strength," Marcus continued, "as things stand now they could swarm all over you. Slice off the Negev in the south, overrun your Galilee settlements in the north, maybe punch through to the coast around Natanya; that's where I'd make my main push if I were in their shoes. As for Jerusalem—"

"Yes?"

"Jerusalem could be strangled."

The massive head snapped back. "Never!"

"I didn't say they'd do it. There are a lot of factors involved. But you asked me for a military opinion. I'm giving it to you—on the basis of the way things stand now, this minute."

Ben-Gurion got up and walked to the window. He stared down for a moment at the white beach and the blue-green Mediterranean, glinting in the bright February sunshine. His eyes, deepset and brown, narrowed in concentration till they were all but lost in the surrounding wrinkles.

He was not entirely surprised at Mickey Marcus's verdict —but he had a long-standing mistrust of "experts." He had heard too many issue the pronouncement, "impossible." He turned back from the window. "You haven't seen our boys fight," he said finally. "Nothing can defeat them."

"You're wrong. I have seen them. And man for man," Mickey went on emphatically, "they're great—the best I've ever seen. Guts—character—imagination. They're a tremendous guerrilla force. But right now they're not an army."

Mickey dragged a chair over to Ben-Gurion's desk and pulled a pad from his pocket. "It's like this," he said, picking up a pencil. "The Haganah is an underground force. With the British running the country, it's had to be. Its main job has been to defend the settlements. And to stage a reprisal now and then—give the Arabs a bloody nose when they stepped too far out of line. So it's been organized— and rightly—as a body of irregulars operating in small units: companies, platoons, even sections of six or eight men."

The pad was being covered with rapid illustrative sketches. "What we face now"—Mickey's shift from "you" to "we" was characteristic, and was to prove a strong factor in endearing him to the Israelis—"is a very different business. The minute the British pull out in the spring, we're going to be hit on every border by modern professional armies: heavily equipped, numerically superior, and organized for large-scale actions. They've been trained by British and French officers not to make a quick stab at a village, but to mount a coordinated offensive, along a front of perhaps a hundred miles . . . to slice off whole territories and isolate enemy forces. How are we going to meet a threat like that? By running Haganah companies up and down the line, trying to plug up every hole as it occurs? It just can't be done!"

Ben-Gurion's fist thumped down on the desk. "Since I came to this country forty-two years ago, people have been telling us 'it can't be done.' So we've gone ahead and done it!"

"Boss—I'm not quarreling with that spirit. It's the greatest asset we've got. I just don't want to see it wasted."

Ben-Gurion sat back heavily. "All right," he said. "I knew we weren't ready. That's why I insisted on getting a man like you over here. Up to now, I've been doing most of the worrying by myself."

Mickey flashed an impish grin. "I'm not much good at worrying. But maybe I can help you attack the problem."

He held up his left hand, fingers spread well apart, before the older man's face. "Haganah is like my hand," he said. "A collection of separate, independent fingers. You can't knock anybody out with one finger"—he gestured to illustrate—"or even with five fingers, used one at a time. What we have to do is knit the separate fingers together" —the fingers tightened into a massive ball—"into one striking fist!"

The knuckles of Mickey's left hand crashed with an emphatic "spat!" into his right palm.

Nothing could have been better calculated to stir Ben-Gurion, the legendary "strong right arm" of Zionism. The veteran political leader lunged forward in his chair.

"So we must learn to attack in powerful formations. That's

what I've been arguing since 1945. How do we do it, Mickey?"

"It's a big order. We need a training program, for one thing, to teach officers strategy, logistics, combined operations. And a staff structure. Then there are supplies, communications . . . and reserves."

"With our shortage of manpower?"

"I know. Most of your commanders think that's a luxury. But it's a necessity. Wars aren't won by just hanging on. After you stop the enemy, you've got to be able to throw in the haymaker for a decision."

Ben-Gurion frowned.

"We'll find a way! Your people have guts, Boss—up to here. They're fighting for a land they've conquered with their own sweat—and a dream they believe in. And you have some excellent young military talent—men like Yadin— Laskov—Dayan—Shamir. And Alon."

Ben-Gurion's eyes measured the American shrewdly. These were, without exception, names he had already earmarked himself. "Good men," he commented. "A couple with staff experience in the British Army. But seldom at higher than company level."

"They can be trained to lead battalions and brigades."

Ben-Gurion reached over and gripped the younger man's arm. He studied the mobile, olive-skinned face: firm chin, generous mouth, broad, football-flattened nose, thick dark brows rising above the intense, glowing black eyes. "Can you help us hammer out an army, Mickey?"

Mickey grinned. "You know I only came here for the swimming." A moment later, soberly: "I couldn't guarantee anything—but I can give it a whirl."

"How long will it take?"

Mickey pursed his lips. "Three months—if we're lucky."

Ben-Gurion stared, nodded, shrugged. "All right, Mickey. How do we start?"

Mickey reached for his brief case. "To begin with—"

Ben-Gurion's phone rang. He picked it up, listened briefly, said a few words in Hebrew. Then he put the phone down and turned to Mickey. "Transport troubles. They want me at a meeting. Can you wait?"

As Ben-Gurion's short, purposeful strides took him from the room, Mick opened his brief case. Inside were a dozen handwritten sheets of notes, several U. S. Army manuals, and a couple of paperback anthologies. He was already accustomed to these interruptions—inevitable in a period of such hectic readjustment—and he had learned to make the most of such moments. He picked out a poetry volume and started thumbing through its well-worn pages.

But for once, the classics were no balm. Mickey put the book away, leaned back in his chair, and closed his eyes.

This was the roughest assignment he had ever taken on. Mickey Marcus had met stiff challenges before: in fact, his life had been a series of them, from the time he was a scrawny kid in Brooklyn, learning to defend himself against neighborhood toughs. He had battered his way into West Point, partly on the strength of a phenomenal high school athletic record. At the Military Academy, he had overcome the trials of a particularly grueling first year and gone on to further sports triumphs, scrambling up from an early-round knockdown to come back and win the intercollegiate welterweight title.

Succeeding years had seen him battle Prohibition mobsters as a Treasury lawyer; smash the underworld rule of the New York City prison system; and organize the first grand-scale movement of American troops overseas in World War II. He had trained city-bred youngsters for the rigors of island fighting against the Japanese, and brought to bear what had been called "the keenest mind in the Pentagon" on the baffling jigsaw of postwar occupation problems.

Mickey Marcus had never held back from a challenge,

especially where an issue of personal principle was at stake. But this time, he knew, the odds against his side were staggering. If wars could be won by sheer power of statistics, the Jews might as well lay down their arms right now. Against six Arab countries outnumbering them in population by sixty to one, and boasting a vast array of modern firearms, they had no tanks, no warplanes, homemade artillery . . . and not even enough rifles to go around. Their frontiers, especially in the south and east, were woefully exposed. Heavily blockaded by the British Navy, they were short of food, fuel, ammunition—in brief, everything except the will to fight.

But they had a cause—a cause for which they were ready, and even eager, to give up their lives. They were defending a land they had rescued with their own hands from barren rocks, a merciless sun, and centuries of neglect. They had created a refuge now desperately needed by their surviving coreligionists in Europe.

Against this, there was pitted a certain Palestinian Arab yearning for freedom from past colonialism. As Mickey saw it, it was a question of two dreams coming to a head-on clash. That of the Jews was older and was held by far more people. What was most important, its fulfillment—right now—was a matter of urgency, not of option.

Palestinian Arabs were free to remain, under improved material conditions, as a political minority in a democratic Jewish republic. If they preferred not to stay, the oil-rich Moslem world outside the Holy Land held vast untapped territories available for immigration.

The Jews snatched from the Nazi slaughterhouses, broken in body and spirit, had no such alternatives. For them, there was no place to go but Palestine; nowhere else where wounds could heal, hope could be fostered, and life slowly be rebuilt in an atmosphere of dignity and self-respect. Mickey remembered vividly the comment of General Lucius

D. Clay, his chief at U. S. Occupation Headquarters in Berlin. General Clay had summed up the view of practically the entire American staff when he said after a visit to a refugee camp: "On the basis of gallantry alone, these people are entitled to a genuine homeland. It's the least the world owes them."

The United Nations had upheld the judgment of the general.

If people far removed from Jewry had such a response, how much stronger must be the determination among the Jews of Israel to keep their country intact, and hold its doors wide open?

Mickey had already seen evidence of that determination. He had witnessed the difference in morale between Ben-Gurion's young night raiders and the superstition-ridden Arab mercenaries who had lately infiltrated across the Palestinian borders. Lifelong "loners," the products of a drowsy feudal culture, the Arabs would fight fiercely, in the tradition of the desert, if cornered hand-to-hand; but they had no instinct for operating together as a disciplined body —and no taste whatever for night fighting.

Unfortunately for the Jews, the regular armies now assembling along their frontiers—especially the troops of Egypt and Transjordan—would be better trained and better led. Nonetheless, the edge held by the Jews in sheer fighting spirit would be there. Mickey Marcus was counting on it heavily. At the moment, there was little else he could count on.

From a strategic point of view, the major headache shaping up was Jerusalem. The historic old capital rose above a rocky crest in the Judean hills, far east of Tel-Aviv, and deep in Arab-surrounded territory. Its only link to the populous coastal strip was by a single winding mountain road, already guarded by an extremely strong complex of enemy positions at the key junction of Latrun, and under constant fire at a dozen other points. Once the real fighting started, it might be impossible to keep that road open. In the absence of an alternate route, the city would be choked off, its hundred thousand Jews at the mercy of the heavy guns that would undoubtedly be hauled across the Jordan by the Transjordan Arab Legion.

Jerusalem, with its large Arab population, would be desperately difficult to defend. Yet its emotional significance made its abandonment unthinkable.

He heard Ben-Gurion's brisk, impatient voice in the corridor outside. "Enough discussion," the Old Man was saying. "Now we must act."

Ben-Gurion entered the room. "Well, Mickey, got everything worked out?"

Mickey caught the rare note of banter in his voice. "Sure, Boss," he replied. "Just one little thing I'll be needing."

"What's that?"

"A miracle. How's your stock holding up?"

The wrinkles settled deeply into the old pioneer's face. "It's never failed us so far," he said soberly. "But we've always met the miracles halfway." He put a hand on Mickey's shoulder. "We've built this country brick by brick, Mickey. We'll defend it the same way."

"Some fellows in New England had the same idea once. It worked for them."

"I've told our Army people what you want to do," Ben-Gurion said. "They're waiting for you downstairs."

Mickey nodded and picked up his brief case. Ben-Gurion walked with him toward the door. "Mickey," he began carefully, "I just heard about you being picked up the other night. We can't afford to have you taking chances like that."

"You've taken a few yourself." Ben-Gurion was famous —or notorious—for disregard of his personal safety.

"Perhaps. But my presence here is not an international secret. Yours is. I want you to promise me—no more poking around the front lines."

"Boss—" Mickey's eyes roamed to the bookcase behind Ben-Gurion. "Better is it that thou shouldest not vow," he intoned, "than that thou shouldest vow and not keep thy word."

Ben-Gurion was startled. "You know Ecclesiastes?"

"One of my favorite authors."

"But I understood you were not a religious man."

"Not in the formal sense."

Ben-Gurion hesitated. He had a huge work load to clear —but this was the kind of discussion he relished.

"What about Zionism?" he pursued. He recalled a fragment of overheard conversation. "Is it true that before you came here you had never heard of Herzl—the founder of the movement?"

Mickey met his intent gaze firmly. "I was at Dachau. The bodies were still piled up like cordwood. After that, I didn't need any more lessons in the importance of a Jewish home-land." Mickey's smile was tight and thin.

Then his lips curled up again, foreshadowing the inevitable grin. "If we're going to do three years of work in three months—I'd better get started."

"All right, Mickey. Let me know what you need." Again Ben-Gurion put his small, expressive hand on Mickey's shoulder. "And please, no unnecessary chances."

"Of course." Again a glance toward the bookcase. " 'A live dog is better than a dead lion.' I know." He waved and was gone.

This was not the first time, Mickey reflected as he stepped out onto the broad, treelined thoroughfare of Rothschild Avenue, that his unusual habits of soldiering had raised headquarters temperatures; four years ago, General John H. Hilldring had been similarly concerned.

Thinking back to that warm spring morning in 1944, Mickey grinned in fond reminiscence. It was over a cup of coffee in the Pentagon, Mickey recalled, that the whole improbable adventure began. . . .

TWO

In the weeks before D-Day, Washington was in many respects the center of the Allied war effort. At the White House, marathon conferences were the order of the day; round-the-clock phone calls across the Atlantic; secret decisions, and top-secret reversals.

Sharing the center of the stage was the sprawling beehive of the Pentagon, its overworked communications channels crackling with bulletins from all points of the compass.

Very near the middle of this gathering typhoon sat the Civil Affairs Division of the War Department, charged with organizing the administration of territories soon to be liberated or occupied. Some three hundred million people—nearly one-sixth the population of the entire globe —were soon to come under the supervision of C.A.D.

It was a situation ripe with possibilities for errors of judgment and angry disputes—two developments that the head of the C.A.D., General Hilldring, was determined to minimize. Hilldring was a blue-eyed, high-domed Regular Army intellectual. As he saw it, the success or failure of his operation hinged largely on his ability to find a Chief of Planning gifted with "the genius to foresee" the vexing legal problems that would arise. Soon after taking over the agency early in 1943, he had sent a signal to Oahu Island in the Pacific requesting the transfer of the man he wanted: Mickey Marcus. In the year of their association, Mickey had become Hilldring's right-hand aide and trusted friend.

One morning Mickey hustled down the long corridor to Hilldring's private office. He dropped a thick sheaf of penciled yellow paper on the general's desk.

"What's this, Mickey?"

"Time Schedule for Norway, Phase One."

Hilldring stared. "But I didn't dump that in your lap till late yesterday. When'd you have time?"

"I had all night, sir."

Hilldring shook his head disbelievingly. "Don't you believe in sleep, Colonel Marcus?"

"Definitely, sir."

"But not when the White House is waiting on the other end of the line, eh?" He picked up the bulky report. "Let's get some coffee."

The fourth-floor snack bar was jammed. Mickey and Hilldring managed to find a stand-up table in a far corner. Mick downed a huge glass of orange juice. "You know, sir, those London queries are going to be coming in faster—and louder. We'll have a full-time job drafting answers . . . let alone thinking."

"What do you suggest we do—suspend communications?"

"No. Improve them."

"How?"

"By having a C.A.D. adviser on the spot. You could do

more in an hour of meetings there than we accomplish in a week of cables."

"Me? To London? Why, the Joint Chiefs have a fit if I go over the state line to Virginia!"

"Then we ought to send someone else," said Mick stubbornly. "Someone who knows the score well enough to do some good."

Hilldring focused sharply on the face before him. Of course. He should have known. Mick was making his semimonthly pitch for an overseas assignment.

The general kept his tone casual. "Well now—who could that possibly be?"

Mick's gaze went up to the ceiling. "I think I could handle the job, sir."

Hilldring noted Mick's close-cropped blue-black hair, the tough bristly stubble on his chin. Everything about the man was taut and alive. And especially those black eyes. Hilldring remembered them from more than one hardpounding conference, burning brightly as if reflecting some unquenchable inner flame.

But now they were merely glinting sparks, throwing out a magnetic force that Hilldring had to rouse himself to resist. "I'll think about it, Mickey. Give me a little more time."

Hilldring's association with Mickey had been a series of surprises, most of them pleasant. He had originally asked for Marcus, then a lieutenant colonel, on the strength of three extravagantly phrased recommendations for Mickey's promotion by successive commanding generals of the Pacific's 27th Division. As divisional Judge Advocate and also Commander of the Ranger School, Mick had acquired a considerable reputation for combining military expediency with legal know-how.

He sounded like exactly what the C.A.D. needed. Hilldring couldn't wait to get him into the Pentagon.

The general was startled, therefore, when a stocky, smiling man in wrinkled cottons sauntered into his office one afternoon and reported for duty with the Government Branch.

The new import didn't dress like a West Pointer. His buttons were unpolished, his sleeves were too long, his tie skewed off at a deplorable angle. Nor did his mild manner suggest the dynamo who had been praised as a legal wizard, organizer, troubleshooter, and all-around answer to a military administrator's dream.

Hilldring's next shock came when Marcus went to work. "'Dynamo" was much too tame. A proposed modification in Greek civil law, bogged down in interoffice memos for two weeks, was cleared for action by Mickey in twenty minutes. A bulging Treasury Department analysis of European economic systems emerged from the Marcus compressor in seven cogent pages.

Where others debated alternatives, he offered solutions; plans for doing, rather than talking, flowed constantly from his desk. When the terms for an Italian surrender were being bounced around the capital like a ping-pong ball, it was Marcus who knifed through to the essence of the problem, and Marcus who sat down and wrote out a simple, comprehensible draft. If the crease in Mickey's trousers might sometimes lack razor-edge sharpness, there was nothing unsoldierly about his mind: it was alert, disciplined, and direct.

The sheer energy of his new aide staggered Hilldring. Mickey frequently put in a sixteen-hour workday, from 8:00 A.M. to midnight. If he quit "early"—at seven or eight in the evening—it was to dash over to the local "Y" for a brisk couple of hours at the giant swing and bar bells (Mick had earned his varsity "A" at West Point for gymnastics as well as boxing).

Coupled with this physical zest was a consistent willingness to tackle anything. Although the dilemmas faced by

C.A.D. in quickly restoring order to war-shattered populations were described as "immeasurable, without dimensions," Hilldring could not remember a single occasion on which Marcus had ducked an assignment with the plea that it was too tough or he was too busy or he wasn't qualified to handle it. Mick operated on the theory that there was an answer to every situation—"nothing just happens, there's always a cause." The trick was to probe until you found the right handle; that might take research, or consultation with a specialist. But once you found the right technique for laying bare the problem, the solution wouldn't be far away.

And now, Hilldring reflected, this deft trouble-shooter was once again asking to be sent overseas. Up to this point, it had been easy enough to dismiss the ingenious proposals that, for "proper implementation," always "required" the presence of Mickey Marcus in one theater of war or another. Marcus was much too valuable a staff officer to send roaming off on dubious "investigations."

But this time, Hilldring had to admit, Mickey had a point. Apart from the possible merits of an on-the-scene C.A.D. survey in Europe after a few towns had been recaptured, there was no doubt that even during the tense preinvasion period, the presence in London of a knowledgeable military government officer from the General Staff would be helpful to the theater commander. And Mickey was unquestionably the coolest head available for the job.

Mickey had earned the trip. And he wanted desperately to go. Hilldring knew that his chief planner's involvement in the war was fierce and personal. Mickey loathed the Nazis and ached to be hurling every sinew in his body against them. Although he never complained openly about being chained to a desk, it was obvious that he chafed under the restraint. The walls of his office were covered with war maps where every pin was shifted with meticulous care to record the changing fortunes of battle.

Hilldring hesitated. Clearly Mickey was more than a little frustrated in his staff-headquarters role. In the Pacific, he had been allowed to train the Rangers for jungle combat but, as Judge Advocate, had not been permitted to follow through with his men and lead them into action against the Japanese. By temperament, training, and personal persuasion, he longed for at least a glimpse of the action. And there was a job to be done in London. . . .

On the other hand, Hilldring liked having Mickey around. Like the Pacific generals before him, he had grown accustomed to relying heavily on Colonel Marcus . . . not just for Mickey's ability to siphon off a big share of the work pressure, but for his engaging, buoyant presence. Who else would be available at any hour of the day or night to give sound legal counsel—or friendly advice on a personal matter? Who else could keep the large and frequently unpredictable staff of C.A.D. civilian advisers in line? Mick, with his unusual blending of government and Army experience, could walk the tightrope between the military and legal-economic worlds.

With faint misgivings, Hilldring summoned a sergeant from the anteroom and told him to prepare travel orders assigning Colonel Marcus to temporary duty at SHAEF, via top-priority air transport departing May 8 for London. Purpose? "To provide liaison, and act as observer in the implementation of military government policies for France."

When Hilldring put the travel papers on Mickey's desk, Mickey didn't say much. He merely grinned—the widest, happiest grin Hilldring had ever seen.

"Better get your gear," Hilldring advised. "Just don't forget where you work."

Mickey saluted. "Cheerio, Boss. And thanks."

Twenty-four hours later, Mickey was in the British capital. Within three days, the number of inquiries directed to C.A.D. began to drop off sharply. In a couple of weeks, the cables were down to a trickle. Hilldring was in a mood of self-congratulation; evidently Mickey was delivering his usual competent performance as a staff officer.

Attention in the Pentagon now shifted to the invasion itself. At long last, the signs were deemed favorable: the tide was right, and the weather outlook no worse than ambiguous. "Overlord" was unleashed against the German-held coast.

While Washington held its breath, the critical moment was reached and successfully passed. The Allies had their foothold in Normandy.

After a week of savage fighting, the bridgehead was secure. D-Day belonged to history.

General Hilldring, leafing through a long memo on the invasion from Chief of Staff George Marshall, became disquietingly aware that he had had no word from his own man in the field since the end of May. He dispatched a cable to Mickey at SHAEF headquarters in London.

There was no answer. A follow-up query elicited the information that Colonel Marcus had parted company with SHAEF some ten days ago; he might possibly be somewhere in Europe.

Hilldring resigned himself to waiting. A second week passed, and then a third—with no sign of Colonel Marcus on the incoming planes from Europe, and no clue as to his whereabouts.

The general was getting angry. What was wrong with his staff? Why hadn't anybody been able to trace Marcus?

For the fourth time, he picked up his phone and asked for a connection with Lieutenant General Walter Bedell Smith, SHAEF Chief of Staff in France. This time he was lucky. Smith had just been talking to General Marshall, and the Pentagon circuit was still open. . . .

"Bedell? This is John Hilldring. Listen—I'm looking for

one of my boys who was detached in London—Colonel Marcus."

"Mickey Marcus? He's over here somewhere, John. Landed with the 101st Airborne."

"He did what?"

"Came in with Max Taylor's outfit, the first day."

"The first—?" Hilldring shook his head. "But that was three weeks ago. Where is he now?"

"I wouldn't know, John. I've got a war on my hands. I can't go playing wet nurse to your colonels."

"I appreciate that, Bedell. But look—can you do me just one favor?"

"What's that?"

"Find Marcus."

"He's been all over the lot, John—"

"Arrest him if you have to—but send him back!"

On his arrival in Europe, Mickey's first move had been to plunge into paper work at headquarters. With his liaison duties securely in hand well before the end of May, Mick set about exploring more interesting matters. He made discreet inquiry about the units that were likely to be employed in the initial invasion wave. A major role, he learned, would go to paratroop forces under Generals Max Taylor and James Gavin.

Maxwell D. Taylor, later Army Chief of Staff, military adviser to President Kennedy and Ambassador to Vietnam, is a tall, spare man who suggests a West Point edition of the late Gary Cooper. He had been a fellow student of Mickey's at the Military Academy. They had not lived in the same barracks, since cadets were at that time grouped by size and Mickey, unlike Taylor, was not within flirting distance of the six-foot marker; but Taylor had pleasant memories of Mickey's boxing-ring prowess and dance-hall exuberance.

Mickey got a warm reception, therefore, when he dropped in at the commanding general's office at the 101st Airborne Division base in Newbury. The personal touch was accented further by Taylor's longtime friendship with Mickey's superior, General Hilldring.

Casually, Mickey hinted that his directive from C.A.D. was very broad, pretty much a matter of his own option. It was Hilldring's idea, he intimated strongly, that the sooner he got into Normandy for direct observation, the better. He assumed that he and his boss could count on General Taylor's co-operation in that regard?

Taylor, more than willing to oblige a couple of old chums, said of course. He would send Mickey along to the proper staff people and they would "set something up"—the usual post-operational distinguished-visitors' tour, complete with jeep and junior officer guide. That, at least, was in Taylor's mind.

But not in Mickey's. He proceeded to the staff meeting armed with the commanding general's blessing, and his own elastic interpretation of his instructions from Washington. As a clincher, he produced a letter of bon voyage from the Assistant Secretary of War.

Obviously, Colonel Marcus expected to ride into France with the invasion forces. But—had he ever made a high-altitude parachute jump? Especially with a heavy combat pack?

Mick waved a careless hand. "I commanded the Ranger School at Oahu." This was perfectly true. But Mick neglected to add that the Ranger course did not include air jumps.

Doubts melted before Mickey's self-confidence. By the end of the meeting, there was agreement in principle that Colonel Marcus would fly in with the first wave of the 101st, if space could somehow be found.

The rest was relatively easy. On D-Day minus one, a young corporal in the 101st, shivering on the windy takeoff strip in

For top-level General Staff services in World War II, Colonel Marcus receives the Distinguished Service Medal on May 18, 1945 from Major General John H. Hilldring in Washington.

A training unit marches toward Jerusalem.

southern England, was herding a group of bulkily-weighted warriors aboard a C-46 transport when Mickey raced up waving a set of papers. The papers were decorated with some of the most impressive signatures in the War Department.

It was not a good moment for extended debate. The peppery little colonel from the Pentagon was squeezed aboard.

Dusk of June 5 had barely given way to a cloudy, brooding night when the skies over the English Channel began to throb with a distant humming. Gradually, the hum swelled to a steady, grinding roar. In the pastureland of Normandy, across from Britain's lower tip, plump cows turned from their grazing and looked up uneasily at the approaching thunder. It was a gesture repeated by a countryside full of German troops, manning anti-aircraft posts and machine guns.

Sweeping toward its objective was the greatest airborne assault force ever assembled—some ten thousand picked troops crowded aboard hundreds of planes and gliders. In all that vast armada were only two men who had never jumped before. One was an Operations officer attached to General Taylor's staff. The other was Mickey Marcus.

At a little past midnight, June 6, 1944, Mickey Marcus sailed in his turn through the open door of the lumbering C-46, feet forward, arms extended, head down. He counted "one thousand, two thousand, three—"

At that moment his chute snapped open and met the full force of the propeller blast. From a speed of 120 miles an hour, he came abruptly to a dead stop. Then the savage "opening shock" was over, and he was falling lightly, easily, eighteen feet per second.

The hum of the airplane motor faded away. He felt peaceful, relaxed. He strained his eyes in the near-moonless dark, trying to make out the landmarks that had been pointed out in his hasty briefing: a heavy stone bridge, a crossroads, a church steeple. None of them was visible: only a thin ribbon of water running among woods and fields.

Mickey could not know it, but nearly every man jumping that night was having a similar problem. The original flight pattern, altered by last-minute intelligence about German troop concentrations, had been further disrupted by thick swirling clouds and enemy anti-aircraft fire. As the formations broke apart, many pilots were deflected to the wrong pathfinder lights. As a result, troopers were drifting down all over the Normandy landscape, with little idea of where they were or who might be next to them.

In the terrain of the Cotentin Peninsula, this last was a considerable headache. The countryside was thick with greenery—tall hedges, orchards, lush meadows—broken up by narrow, winding lanes and drainage ditches. A hedge might be full of roses, brambles—or Germans. And once the hedge started firing, it was too late.

Mick came down in an open field. He executed the shock-breaking landing tumble without effort. Once on the ground, he pressed the quick-release box on his chest, detaching the four points of his parachute, and shucked off the harness. He unslung his automatic rifle. Everything was in good shape.

He examined the terrain before him. Directly ahead, to the north by his wrist compass, he could make out the dim outline of a New England-type stone boundary wall, and beyond that some farm buildings. At his left was a long row of hedges; behind him, the trees. To the right and in the distance was a slope that might lead to a drainage ditch.

There was a thud to his left.

Mick flattened out.

Dead silence.

Mick wheeled his automatic around. Carefully, trigger finger at the ready, with the other hand he took a small object from his pocket and squeezed it. The shrill chirp of a cricket pierced the stillness.

A moment's pause—and then an identical chirp came from his left, repeated rapidly. Mick breathed easier. There were no live crickets in Normandy. SHAEF had distributed thousands of toy soundmakers, reproducing the effect of a male cricket scraping his forewings, as a device for enabling the invaders to signal each other. Mick crawled forward cautiously.

Out of the darkness loomed the shape of a man—a husky young paratrooper with a sergeant's stripes. An exchange of muffled, warm greetings and Colonel Marcus was in business. He had the beginnings of a combat team.

In the next three hours, additional ghostly shapes floated down—paratroopers of all ranks from a haphazard assortment of units. Using the clump of trees as a temporary cover, Mick organized the makeshift force into two patrols, one headed by himself, the other by a major from Intelligence.

They were apparently several miles from the nearest of the pre-arranged assembly points. As a misty dawn crept over the fields, Mick sent the major's patrol southward to probe for a linkup with similar lost detachments. With his own group, he headed toward the now distinguishable cluster of farm buildings.

They had barely moved into the open when a burst of fire slashed across the meadow. There was indeed, as Mick had surmised, a drainage ditch far off to the right; and a Nazi machine gun crew was planted there.

Mick made a rapid survey of the terrain. His first problem was to get within closer range of the enemy nest. A broken row of low shrubs offered fair protection for some fifty yards. After outlining his plan of action to the patrol, Mick dropped to his belly. In single file behind him, the patrol crawled toward the German gun post.

At the end of the trail, Mick opened fire with his automatic rifle. The German gun swung around to answer him. Shifting position along the hedge as he blazed back, Mickey nodded to his sergeant to swing the rest of the men down a nearby embankment, then take them in a wide flanking movement toward the enemy rear. He would keep the gunner tied up.

And he did, twice slithering out into the open behind a boulder and a tree stump to change his angle of fire. It was a classic demonstration of combining fire and movement. The exasperated Germans, totally preoccupied with Mickey's murderous sharpshooting, were helpless when the patrol swooped down on them from behind.

By that time, scores of local engagements had broken out in the area. If the wide dispersion of the landings had created problems of regrouping for the Americans, it had also brought them an unexpected benefit: the baffled Germans thought they were being hit from the air by six divisions, rather than elements of two.

Now motorized Nazi reserves were speeding along the roads, while foot patrols explored every farmyard and orchard. The hedges were alive with snipers. There was no fixed front; only battles of maneuver between small and often leaderless groups.

One such party of roaming paratroopers had Mickey to thank for a narrow escape. Hearing cricket sounds on the other side of a cowshed, the Americans had started confidently forward when Mickey halted them with a whispered command. The chirps, he had noticed, were spaced slowly and clumsily, as if by someone unacquainted with their usual sound. Playing a hunch, Mick ordered the troopers to break into three groups and encircle the area.

They did—and captured a band of German riflemen holding several American prisoners. The Germans had been using the cricket-sounders found on the Americans as bait—ingeniously, but not ingeniously enough.

In those first wild days of fighting, Mick slipped in and out of a dozen other encounters. As the campaign progressed, legends began to circulate about a Civil Affairs colonel who bounced through the countryside, here joining a combat outfit for a couple of days, there lingering in a newly occupied village to help set up a military government.

Mickey was finally discovered and was hustled aboard a plane for London; and then, still in his combat woolens, was transferred to a States-bound transport aircraft. Mickey's march on Berlin was over, at least for the moment.

The final evaluation of Mickey's Normandy interlude did not come until nearly a year later, when he was awarded a Distinguished Service Medal. The official citation noted among other things, "the first-hand experience acquired in accompanying the 101st Airborne Division in the invasion of Normandy," which led to "important modifications in policies and procedures" for the Civil Affairs Division.

Beyond medals and heroics, Normandy was a key episode in the reaffirmation of Mickey's character, the strongest expression yet of his determination to live his beliefs without compromise.

This devotion to idealistic impulse rested on a firm moral base. But it was backed by something more: the knowledge that whatever he did, his wife Emma would be there, accepting his decision.

What price Emma paid for her generosity is another matter. But she enabled Mickey to pursue his moonbeans; and this was no small factor in the forces that, three and a half years after the liberation of France, drew him to a small seaside hotel in gravely troubled Tel-Aviv.

THREE

Tel-Aviv, Israel.   *Feb. 16, 1948*

Dearest Snippy,

I am about to go on a mission. The task seems so gigantic.
No one man can do this job; were there 50 men here trained
at staff level, perhaps that would be enough.

Yet, one has to dig some earth before an Empire State
building is erected. I shall think only of the individual cu-
bicles and perhaps an edifice may arise. . . .

I have yet to see anywhere in the world so inspiring a group
as the children of Palestine—I mean "children" from 3 to 23.
What a spirit—what energy—unspoiled, eager to learn, cour-
teous, serious, understanding, alive to the situation, fearless
and in a true sense, modest.

They are physically and mentally a new breed of men. Yes,
a different kind of Jew is being born; and if the baby is not
to perish, all the help that America can give must be given
NOW. The problem is difficult only because the needed support is denied to them.

"Help!" It seems all the world looks to America. All others come alive only when America smiles on them.

Mick glanced up from the writing pad cradled in his lap. He sat outside his hotel room on a small curved balcony. Below him lay the Mediterranean. Moments before, Mick had watched as the huge glowing sun sank slowly into the metallic waters of the sea.

Now it was night. To his left, on the south, the picturesque jumble of ancient Arab Jaffa was dissolving into a dim outline of shore and minaret. Far out at sea a light winked on, first of the night fishing fleet.

Returning to his room, Mickey sat down at the writing desk to reread his note. No day went by when he did not thus reaffirm his lifeline to the girl who waited in Brooklyn. It was a habit that began the day he arrived at training camp in Alabama in 1940, and it was kept up without a break, except where the fortunes of warfare prohibited, throughout his globally scattered seven years of Army service.

He reached into the desk drawer for an envelope, and printed carefully on the back the unfamiliar name "Michael Stone, Gat Rimmon Hotel. . . ."

Folding the note, he had an afterthought. He opened it again and added under his signature:

We shall have victory!
I doubt if I have ever done anything—anywhere—any time —that is more worthwhile and that you too, perhaps—in spite of the sacrifices on your part—will look upon with more satisfaction. It is a necessary job and we shall be rewarded somehow. I am completely content that my reward will be just living and being with you.

Mickey sealed the letter and leaned back. Facing him on the desk was a leather folder containing two small photos of Emma, sent to him in Germany in 1945 when he complained that he had no recent pictures of her. The photos were vividly lifelike, capturing almost too well Emma's features: the pert nose, faintly Oriental cheekbones, cool smiling eyes, the sweetly curved lips.

Mickey sighed.

It had not been easy, this latest parting. He had come home from the wars at last in the spring of 1947. Not only Normandy and the Pacific were behind him, but a subsequent hurly-burly of travels and conferences beginning in the summer of 1944: Dumbarton Oaks, Quebec, and Yalta; Potsdam and the Allied Control Council for Germany; Italy and Scandinavia. Ready early in 1946 for a well-earned return to civilian life, he was instead requested by the Pentagon to take over as Chief of its War Crimes Branch—leading to still another round of journeys through Europe and Asia as he recruited personnel for the trials at Nuremberg and in the Orient.

Already in 1945, in a letter to Emma from Berlin, anticipating an end to his wanderings, he had listed some of the innumerable stopovers recorded in flying the equivalent of three times around the earth (and he was to fly some sixty thousand miles more). His 1945 letter commented: "Yes, many heartaches and pains. It has been just as tough on you—perhaps MORE than on me. But perhaps we shall have a better social order in the world."

Even after the "one-last-assignment" of Nuremberg, the Army did not relinquish Mickey's services easily. As a final inducement to keep him in khaki, the Pentagon came through at long last with the prize that had eluded Mickey for many years: his general's star.

As a brigadier general, Mickey would round out his military career with a proper flourish—and achieve the dream nursed by the lowliest of West Point plebes from the moment of sighting the turreted magnificence of the Military Academy.

Along with Mickey's promotion would go the much-coveted post of military attaché at the United States Embassy in Moscow. All he had to do was stay in uniform.

It was a tempting proposition. Against it stood only a handful of promises to Emma—and to himself.

The temptation lasted about twenty minutes. Mick had already devoted to the Army the best part of a decade. He had won (although he never wore) a chestful of decorations, including the Distinguished Service Medal, the Bronze Star, Honorary Knight Commander of the British Empire, and seven others. At forty-five, there were other aspects to living. It was time to call a halt.

And so in the early spring of 1947 David Marcus, private citizen and attorney, came back to Brooklyn. His first act was to get a house large enough for the substantial household that had accumulated around Emma as a result of the wartime shortage of apartments, coupled with the traditional Marcus open-door policy for family members.

Mickey settled on a two-story frame house on Westminster Road in Brooklyn, along a quiet oak-lined street in a neighborhood of thick grassy lawns and wide front porches. It had a lantern glowing at the door, a swing rocking on the porch, and the cosy residential atmosphere peculiar to Old Flatbush. With its high windows and unexpected alcoves, it was a comfortable place to come home to.

Mick shucked off his Eisenhower jacket, filled his long-empty wardrobe with a stack of civilian suits, and started casting about for law office space in crowded Manhattan.

His return was greeted by a flood of friendly letters: from Governor Thomas E. Dewey, who had been a young government prosecutor with Mickey; and such other dignitaries of his profession as Judges John C. Knox, Simon Rifkind, A. David Benjamin, and Thomas Downs.

Desk space was finally provided by Mickey's old crony, Jules "Indian" Yablok, the onetime all-American halfback from Colgate, who had a law office at 545 Fifth Avenue. Mickey set about methodically building up a law practice.

New York not having a shortage of lawyers, major cases did not tumble into Mickey's lap overnight. But gradually, as summer turned to fall, the corporate clients and the large fees were beginning to come his way.

That was where matters stood on the December afternoon when a short, chesty man of erect bearing walked through the door to Yablok's suite and asked to see Colonel Marcus.

Mickey looked up from the desk where he was chatting with an old Army buddy, Lieutenant Colonel Morton Strauss. "I'm Mickey Marcus. What can I do for you?"

The stranger turned a pair of earnest blue eyes in Mickey's direction. "My name is Shamir. I am here on behalf of the Provisional Jewish Government in Palestine."

The ears of the two Americans pricked up. Establishment of a Jewish State in the Middle East had been voted by the United Nations some ten days before.

"Have a chair, Mr. Shamir."

The visitor corrected Mick politely: "Major Shamir."

"Sorry," Mickey leaned forward intently, his interest heightened. "Yes, Major?"

Shamir came directly to the point. The Jews of Palestine at long last had the blessings of the international community for their state. But blessings might not be enough. The U.N. had declined to take measures for the implementing of its partition resolution, despite open Arab threats to nullify it in the spring by overwhelming invasion. The Jews were thus forced back upon their own defensive strength—namely, the underground Army called Haganah—which they were beginning to suspect might be quite inadequate to handle the expected full-scale assault.

Shamir, who had risen to the rank of major in the British Army during World War II, had been given the mission of recruiting in America a military expert or a group of experts who could survey the needs of the Jewish forces and make some broad recommendations. American Zionist authorities had advised Shamir that ex-Colonel Marcus, with his wide acquaintance in Army circles, might be able to help him find the right man.

Mick pondered a few seconds, then cracked his fist emphatically into his palm. "I think I've got the guy for you!" He called out to his secretary: "Elsie! See if you can get General—no, never mind, hold it." He turned back to Shamir. "This is too important to handle by phone. Can you come to San Francisco?"

"When?"

"Right now."

Shamir brightened. "Of course." He had been told Marcus moved fast—but he was not prepared for anything like this.

Mickey swung around to Strauss. "What about you, Moishe? You got anything on the agenda bigger than nailing down a homeland for the Jews?"

"Well, when you put it that way, Mick—"

Mick's high tenor crackled across the room. "Okay, Elsie, call La Guardia Field. Three tickets for San Francisco, the first plane we can catch! Then call my home and leave word for Mrs. Marcus that I've had to go out of town for a couple of days. I'll phone her late tonight." Mickey sat back, alive with satisfaction, like a veteran prize fighter who hears the roar of the crowd outside his dressing room and can already feel the rubbery canvas of the ring under his feet.

Some four days later, just as the midnight news broadcast was ending, a cab door slammed shut outside the house in Flatbush and Mickey's light, quick step sounded on the porch steps. Emma, listening to the radio in the darkened bedroom, hurried downstairs. She found Mickey tiptoeing uncertainly among the pots and pans, in obvious search of coffee. She kissed him, sat him down at the table, and in a few graceful, long-legged strides had refreshments under way. Now, what was this "international case" he had been so guarded about over the long-distance phone?

Mick told her about the appeal for help from Shamir, and his "hunch" that the retired major general on the West Coast might be the answer.

And how did his inspiration work out?

"Great start, bum ending." Over a cup of steaming black coffee, Mickey explained. The general had at first been much taken with the idea, and Shamir had been equally taken with the American's credentials. Shamir had been on the point of cabling a tentative report to Ben-Gurion, when the general interposed his single reservation: He did not wish to jeopardize his pension status as a retired Regular Army officer. If that detail could be ironed out. . . .

Mickey had jumped into the breach, volunteering to sound out the powers concerned in Washington. For two days he had buttonholed old friends in Pentagon corridors and banged on doors that he would never have approached for a favor on his own behalf. He encountered lots of sympathy—but no guarantees about the pension.

And so the general's misgivings remained. For a time the proposition hung in mid-air, while compromises were sought. But it refused to jell, and finally, inevitably, it had disintegrated. "The Jews are right back where they were four days ago, Snippy. Six hundred thousand people in search of a military adviser."

Emma patted his shoulder. "You've done all you could," she said gently.

"But it wasn't enough. The situation is worse than I told you—I mean, the military position of the Jews. I've done a little talking with Shamir. I have a hunch there's no Jewish Army at all, in the proper sense. They stand to be overrun, simply smashed, if they're hit by complete brigades and divisions loaded with modern British equipment. Do you realize what that means, Snippy—for those displaced persons in Europe—and for the U.N.?"

Mickey got up and began to pace restlessly. "It's all wrong, Snippy. Here we've finally put the Fascists and Tojo out of business. We're founding a new social order based on justice —liberty—the great values of the American Revolution. We establish a community of nations to replace the old rule of force. And what happens the very first time that community takes collective action? Force is going to come in again, through the back door. Then what was all the fighting for?"

Emma knew of Mickey's deep commitment to the United Nations; the hours of research and debate he had put in helping to hammer out its principles at Dumbarton Oaks, and the follow-up committee meetings he had attended in London. A recurrent theme of his letters and conversations since the beginning of the war had been the need for a more integrated relationship among peoples, embodied in a strong international organization. He saw the United States as the natural leader of such a movement.

"There's another angle that can't be overlooked," Mickey went on, "although the British are doing a good job of trying. I mean the way the Jews of Palestine pitched in on the Allied war effort. There were thousands of them fighting on our side in Europe and Africa and the Middle East, while Farouk and his buddies were sulking in their palaces."

"And the Mufti was making speeches for Hitler in Berlin," added Emma. "Of course it's wrong. But how much more can we do about it?"

"Aren't the Jews entitled to a share in the victory—a land they can call their own?"

"After all, Mick, the U.N. did finally vote in favor of a Jewish State—"

"Sure, they voted. That's like passing an ordinance against

housebreaking, but neglecting to provide a police department." He shook his head, fuming. "It's just too ironic. We
smash the Axis, at God knows what cost in lives. We sweat
out a United Nations Organization that's supposed to outlaw
aggression, defend human rights, protect small states as well
as large. We decide by democratic vote to restore a persecuted
people to their homeland.

"And then—" Mickey snapped his fingers—"we undo the
whole thing. At the first yap of defiance—the first real test—
we're looking the other way. We're saying in effect, It's okay,
fellas, we didn't really mean all that stuff about stopping aggression. Not if you handle it right." He came to a pause
before Emma and faced her earnestly. "It's no good, Snippy.
Somebody's got to do something."

"Who, Mickey? You? Is that what you're trying to say—
that you want to go to Palestine?"

Mickey looked at her, startled, as if unaware that the idea
had even entered his mind. "Me?" He got up from the table
and put his arms around her. "No, Snippy. I've been away
too much already. There are other people around. I'll find
an answer to this thing. I've got to."

He trotted up to the bedroom. In five minutes his head
was on the pillow, and seconds later he was asleep, his face
calm and untroubled.

Not so Emma. The signs were all too plain to her: the
stirrings of those forces deep within Mickey that guided, as
if by remote control, his most fundamental decisions.

In the next ten days, Mickey had several more meetings
with Shamir, clarifying for himself the exact picture in
Palestine. He learned that the Jewish underground had no
real artillery, only a handful of small, short-range infantry
mortars. Its air power was nil. Its guerrillas fought mostly
with locally manufactured short-range Sten guns, supplemented by rifles, grenades, and some carefully hoarded light
machine guns. All arms, being illegal, had to be locked away

from British searching parties when not in active use for repelling Arab raids. Operationally, Haganah took the field as platoons, or at most fought in company strength. Its leadership was largely veterans of the Jewish Brigade, untrained in planning broad-scale actions because their British commanders in World War II had no intention of equipping them with knowledge that might one day be turned against England.

Shamir's instructions from Tel-Aviv listed only six potentially acceptable candidates in the United States. Although Mickey's name was among them, Shamir did not tell him so. Haganah as an underground was wary of strangers—many of its members had survived European imprisonment only by being ultraconscious of security—and Mickey's lack of previous connection with Zionism was not reassuring. Instead, Shamir launched cautious inquiries into Mickey's character.

Meanwhile, he enlisted Mickey's help in tracking down the others on his list. The results were not cheering. Two senior officers were away. One had just accepted a top industrial post. Another pleaded excessive fatigue.

A handful of volunteers did come forward, mostly Zionists of long standing; but Mick had to agree with Shamir's abrupt judgment that while such men might ultimately be useful assistants, they were simply not qualified for the top post.

The confidential reports on Colonel Marcus, on the other hand, were piling up a fairly irresistible case, hardly weakened by the growing intimacy between the two men. Not only were all roads beginning to point to Mickey; there was not so much as a dirt track pointing anywhere else.

In mid-January, Mickey and Shamir were joined at lunch by Moshe Sharett, Political Representative of the Jewish Agency and the ranking Palestinian in the United States. Their talk continued well into the afternoon.

That night at home, Mick was unusually quiet. After dinner, when Emma sat down at the piano, he did not stretch out on the couch to savor Chopin as usual, but retired to a reading nook off the living room. Emma recognized the fat volume under his arm as James Truslow Adams' *History of the United States*.

It was nearly two hours before he slammed the book shut and came upstairs. "Snippy—they want me to go to Palestine."

Emma turned from her dressing table. The comb she was trailing through her long dark hair came slowly to a halt. "What did you tell them?"

"I said it couldn't be just my decision. I'd have to talk to you first."

"But you want to go?"

Mickey walked to the window and stared out at the frosty night. "I'd hate to turn them down," he said finally. He turned to his wife earnestly. "This country was settled by fugitives from religious oppression, Snippy!" He held out the Adams book, as if entering an exhibit in court. "What if everybody had abandoned the colonials? Where would George Washington have been without help—French arms, Haym Solomon's money, Lafayette and Von Steuben and Kosciusko?"

Mickey stopped. A tear was trickling down his wife's cheek. He hurried to embrace her. "Snippy, darling. Don't."

"What do you expect me to do—cheer?"

"I wouldn't have to be away long."

"It isn't just that. It's . . . how little I mean to you."

"Snippy!" Mickey's voice took on an unnatural emotional edge. "Never say that. Never, never. If I feel strongly about these things it's mainly because of you—for you—for the things we both believe in!"

He kissed her gently.

"Why must it always be you, Mickey? There are other men

who believe in freedom and still manage to preserve some personal life. Look at your friend—"

"I can't answer for other men, Snippy. I have to live with myself."

"And run off from home every time somebody shouts for help? There'll always be people in trouble, Mickey. You can't put the world straight by yourself. Are you going to fight in Bulgaria and China and Argentina every time somebody steps on one of your ideals?"

"It's not only a matter of ideals, Snippy. It's people . . . I never talked to you much about Dachau."

"I wouldn't let you. I had enough nightmares from the newsreels."

"The newsreels didn't begin to tell it. I climbed over mountains of corpses, Snippy. Schoolboys and young girls and mothers still clutching their infants. . . ."

Emma's mind went back to a stark phrase in a letter written from Germany after Mickey had been inspecting refugee camps: "It seemed to me there were no young Jews left."

Now Mickey was talking about the survivors. "They had only one hope, Snippy, one dream. Sitting there in rags, still behind barbed wire, they talked and they sang and they planned about Palestine. Where else? They saw no future in wandering over Europe again. They could hardly stay in Germany, where the smell of death was still hanging in the breeze. The only security those European Jews could see was in a state of their own, in setting down roots. And who's to say they're wrong—that is, if we really believe everybody is entitled to life, liberty, and the pursuit of happiness? You can't pursue happiness if you don't belong anywhere, and if you haven't got a place that belongs to you."

"But all these years, Mickey—you're never been a Zionist."

"It isn't a question of labels, Snippy. We committed ourselves to a job: not just finishing off Hitler, but building a decent peace. And I hate to walk away from a job half-done."

"But you have no trouble walking away from me."

"No trouble! Snippy, have a heart! Don't break me in half, will you?" Mickey sat down wearily on the bed. "Let's let it go for a while, Sweets. I told them there wouldn't be any answer for at least a couple of days."

Long into the night Emma lay awake, reflecting on Mickey's words, trying to disentangle her own conflicting emotions.

She had married a do-gooder, and in her heart of hearts she was proud of it. Mickey brought the gift of love to a world in which it had always been in notoriously short supply. He conceived of liberty and democracy as dynamic forces, not to be coddled by a warm fireside and protected against the chill night air, but able to survive only if they could spread freely everywhere.

Looking at the society around her, Emma had to admit that Mickey stood virtually alone, like a solid oak in a field of scrub. Not comfort was his banner, but a belief in the potential of the individual. It would be a sad day for humanity if the time should ever come when there would be no Mickey Marcuses left to lead its thankless struggles; when all men, not merely most, were content to sink down beneath their personal barricades of indifference and selfishness and complacency.

She felt a sudden joy in being part of Mickey, as he was part of her. An enigma he might be, with dizzying turns of fancy that she could not understand and impulses at whose deeply-hidden sources she could only guess; but an enigma that she loved.

"Hey, Snippy! What cooks?" Mick stood in the doorway of the bedroom the next morning. "You going somewhere, baby?"

"Not me," said Emma, unlocking the suitcase that lay on the bed, "you. Do you want your tan jacket? They say it's cold in the hills of Jerusalem."

Mickey grinned, relaxing. That "special" quality he counted on in his Snippy had come through for him again. He came into the room. "Can't wait to get rid of me, eh?"

"That's right." Emma turned her head away. "I just—can't wait."

Mick caught the break in her voice. He pushed aside the suitcase and took her in his arms. "It won't be for long, Snippy. Ol' Doc Marcus will find out what ails 'em—write out a prescription—and come flying right back. You'll hardly know I've been gone. Come on, Snippy. Chin up."

She raised her head obediently, and he kissed her.

When, Emma thought to herself wearily, will they start striking off medals for the wives?

If Mickey would not move without his wife's approval, he was equally adamant about securing the blessings of his Uncle Sam. Unlike the general in San Francisco, he was not concerned with possible financial loss; but in no circumstances —whatever the crisis in Palestine—was he willing to compromise the safety or basic welfare of the United States.

In his own view, there was no real clash of interests involved: By aiding the United Nations-sponsored Jewish republic he would be strengthening the forces of democracy, and enhancing American prestige in an area of considerable importance to the West. But he had to be sure that Washington did not disagree. So he let the word filter through to the Pentagon as well as to certain civilian policymakers that he was planning a Middle Eastern trip to survey the military needs of the embattled Jews and offer his counsel.

Back came the answer, via a carefully chosen intermediary: So long as Mickey acted discreetly, going about his business without flaunting his U.S. Army background or his past government connections; so long as he made it clear that his

presence and his advice were strictly personal and unofficial—
there was no objection.

One highly placed official went further. In a private phone
call from the capital, he hailed Mickey's decision as being in
the highest tradition of soldierly patriotism ("Lafayette would
have been on your side, Mickey"), and requested Mickey to
file with him on returning a confidential appraisal of the
military picture, for scrutiny by U.S. intelligence authorities.

Would Mickey have offered himself with equal fervor on
behalf of threatened Czechs or Nigerians or Koreans? Perhaps. The fires of freedom burned deep and strong within
him. The suffering he had seen—certain to have stirred a far
more callous and unimaginative heart than his—might have
been just as moving in a different setting and with different
victims.

But there was a unique element at Dachau. The corpses
Mick had gazed upon were Jews . . . Jews only a few decades
separated from his own parents, who had sought refuge in
America from just such horrors. Many of the pitiful skeletons
who returned his stares, too weak for speech, were his own
contemporaries. Like many a Jew before and after him,
Mickey must have experienced the nerve-tingling thought,
"There but for the grace of God go I."

Two last-minute items remained to be cleared with
Haganah. As a precaution against embarrassing American
relations with the British, Mickey insisted on using a
pseudonym. The day before the flight, a messenger delivered
to his home a neat set of papers identifying him as "Michael
Stone."

Finally, he would not accept any salary.

On a raw, somber afternoon just before the end of January 1948, Emma's brother, Alfred A. Chaison, pulled up
his car before the modest cocoa-brown house in Flatbush.
Emma got in with Mickey and Shlomo Shamir.

The road to La Guardia Airport was icy, and the landscape bleak. Nobody had much to say.

At 5:15 P.M., Mick held Emma to his chest for a sudden
fierce, clinging moment—whispered that he'd make up for
everything when the fight was won—and ran up the ramp. A
few minutes later the plane took off into a thickening darkness.

FOUR

At first glance, the not-quite crystallized Jewish republic shaped up as a kind of miniature California; a Golden State scaled down to the size of Vermont. Like its sprawling American counterpart, it was a land of abundant sunshine and brief winter rains; of oranges and vineyards, and populous cities along its sea-flanked western edge; of spiny inland mountain ranges encasing lush valleys in the north and broiling badlands in the south.

Its major city, the overnight wonder of Tel-Aviv, was a tightly packed edition of balmy Los Angeles, without the smog. A couple of hours' drive north brought you to breeze-blown Haifa, the San Francisco of the Middle East, commanding from the slopes of Mount Carmel a magnificent bay view that lacked only the Golden Gate Bridge. And on the other side of the central mountain range, like the California capital of Sacramento, stood ancient Jerusalem.

The comparison was inescapable—but militarily mislead-
ing. For one thing, the entire territory held by the Jews could
have been tucked away in the State of Massachusetts—an
area small enough for a modern armored force to overrun
in a matter of days. At one spot, in a neck of land below
Haifa, the country was no more than ten miles wide. Its
population was mainly in the plains, and in fact more than
half of its six hundred thousand people lived in the narrow
coastal strip; the fertile inland plateaus were few and widely
scattered, and the pioneering settlements in the south even
more so. The land, until more water could be brought in to
counteract centuries of neglect, was largely blank and hard
and inhospitable.

But the biggest point of difference was the sea of Arabs
within which the tiny Jewish state would be marooned. On
its borders stood a swarm of populous, socially backward and
highly inflammable countries whose rulers had sworn to de-
stroy the Jewish republic.

True, the Arabs were divided. Mick was aware that the
Arab chieftains were not unanimous in wanting war in Palestine, and that in fact the campaign against the Jews was
spurred largely by two men: the Grand Mufti of Jerusalem,
and King Abdullah, puppet ruler of British-dominated
Transjordan.

Thus far, Arab intervention had been relatively unorgan-
ized. The Arabs, like the southerners in the American Civil
War, regarded themselves as a great military people. They
assured each other that irregular Arab forces would be more
than enough to vanquish the Jewish "nation of shop-keepers."

They would learn differently, but they were committed
much too deeply to turn back. The Arab League had proclaimed to the world that there would be "a Jewish massacre";
they would "sweep the Zionists into the sea." For the sake
of their prestige at home and in the world, the Egyptians
and Syrians and all the others would be forced to succeed,

or try to. And they had tremendous forces available to do the job—forces that on paper, at least, could swamp overnight the scattered fragments of brigades that the Zionists could put into the field.

Already the Jews were feeling the pressure of attempting to defend themselves against Palestinian Arabs who outnumbered them two to one, and whose villages straddled Jewish communication lines in every sector of the country.

The immediate Arab goal was to isolate the Jewish settlements and then starve them out. In the south, the tiny settlements of the virtually roadless Negev could be encircled and strangled at leisure.

The Arabs had struck the moment the United Nations voted its partition plan on November 29, 1947. Within a few hours, Palestinian Arabs under the direction of the Grand Mufti were burning and looting shops in the Jewish districts of Jerusalem. The Mufti's snipers and ambush crews were soon reinforced by irregular "volunteers" pouring across the border from Transjordan, Syria, and Iraq. This "Arab Liberation Army" was headed by the German-speaking Fawzi el Kaukji, a Lebanese soldier of fortune who had been active in the anti-Jewish riots of 1936, and who was a trusted friend of both the Grand Mufti and the Nazis.

Against this array, the Haganah could muster only half of the Arab numerical strength: the three thousand full-time soldiers of the crack Palmach, backed by several thousand front-line forces of the Chish or Haganah Field Army. The bulk of the Chish brigades were still in the process of mobilization, as was the entire reserve body of older "Chim" or Home Guard troops. The Jewish arms shortage was acute. The staple weapon was a homemade Sten gun of skimpy fifty-yard range and erratic trajectory. The 2nd Carmeli Brigade of Chish had rifles for only one-third of its men.

Complicating the Haganah's plight was the presence of the "neutral" British, who methodically confiscated Jewish

arms and broke up Jewish attacks, while beaming benevo-
lently upon the Arab bases being established under their
noses.

The deterioration of British-Jewish relations had been one
of the sad ironies of the Palestinian muddle. Britain had
been the first influential advocate of the Zionist cause;
Englishmen like Lord Balfour had been the staunchest pro-
ponents of a Middle Eastern Jewish homeland.

Unfortunately, their idealistic intentions had been placed
in the hands of Colonial Office administrators. Fanned by
considerations of oil, latent anti-Semitism in the Colonial
Office shot to the surface, to receive a powerful assist from
the incoming Foreign Secretary of the 1945 Labor Government, Ernest Bevin. The situation had hardly been improved
by Britain's failing colonial fortunes in the postwar world, or
by the occasional extremist-underground violence against
politically disinterested British soldiers.

By 1948, the frustrated British military command in
Palestine, with a few notable exceptions, was openly pro-
Arab. In this situation, the Jews could only try to push their
makeshift armored cars through the Arab net, and make
limited reprisal raids on villages used as bases for operations.
With British tanks hovering over the scene, large-scale Jewish
actions were out of the question—even if Haganah had been
equipped to carry them out.

What worried Mickey most was that the Jewish Army was
far from being so equipped. Although broad strategic plans
existed, its commanders were not trained in big-formation
tactics. And there was also the problem of centralized command. In theory, Palmach was a subordinate branch of
Haganah; the assault wing or "spearhead" subject to the directions of the Haganah Chief of Staff. In practice, through
its isolated training centers and the grim comradeship of its
night raids, Palmach had become a world unto itself. Its
leadership was native-born; its spirit so strong that the "spear-

head" did not always obey the orders of the loose military-political command centered in Tel-Aviv. Mickey decided to throw his weight immediately behind Ben-Gurion's effort to develop an efficiently organized modern army.

FIVE

Springtime came early to Palestine in 1948. Over the hill-sides, olive trees spread their shimmering mantle, lacy and silver green. In the fields, wild poppies blazed among cyclamens of soft azure blue.

And on the road from Tel-Aviv to Jerusalem, the blood ran red.

Elsewhere the Arabs were being more or less held at bay. El Kaukji's "Liberation Army" in the north, during the month since its arrival in mid-February, had launched two frontal assaults—the usual attack maneuver of the irregulars. A lunge toward Haifa had been thrown back; another against a Jordan Valley settlement had ended in fiasco. Nor had the Arabs fared much better in the Negev, where a single widely-scattered Jewish battalion was still squeezing supplies through to isolated settlements, despite the Moslem Brotherhood blockade.

But in the center, where the Mufti's Palestinian troops had been reinforced by volunteer elements from across the borders, the position of the Jews had become desperate. The thin lifeline from the coast to Jerusalem, threading through thirty miles of enemy-held territory, was all but closed. Convoys attempting to run the gauntlet were suffering terrible losses, and several times had been wiped out altogether. The British, responsible under the mandate for keeping the roads clear, had given up all pretense of doing so. They contented themselves with pushing through their own supplies from time to time, in armored-car convoys much too strong to be challenged by either side.

In American geographical terms, it was as if Washington, D.C. stood at the top of a circling mountain road, besieged from Baltimore and Virginia, with New York as its only source of supply and the enemy controlling the area in between.

The most brutal segment of the journey to Jerusalem was the Bab-el-Wad ravine, a narrow highway slithering snake-like between high stony walls from the foothills east of Tel-Aviv to the first soaring plateaus of the Judean mountains.

Bab-el-Wad—"Gateway to the Valley"—was a perfect man-trap, cruelly designed by nature as if to accommodate Arab ambush. Its wild craggy slopes, where giant boulders mingled with thick eucalyptus trees and the ruins of ancient fortresses, offered a thousand hiding places from which snipers could fire down on traffic trying to squeeze through the pass below.

The great stones and heavy trees also provided the Arabs with easy roadblocks; two or three were enough to choke the tight passage completely. The moment the Jews left their homemade armored cars to remove the obstacles, they came under merciless fire from men they could not see.

To accentuate the nightmare, the continual twists and hairpin curves in the ditch-bordered road restricted the field of vision of the convoy drivers to a few yards at a time.

On March 5, Mick wrote Emma a somber letter from Tel-Aviv, where the shops were still bustling with activity and nighttime crowds overflowed the brightly lighted street cafés:

All this is such a contrast to what I experienced yesterday returning from a trip to Jerusalem. There is a stretch of road between Jerusalem and Tel-Aviv, about fifteen miles in length, that is called the Bloody Road. Every day Jews are killed as their convoys rush past.

The British do nothing. Yet the Jews must keep that road open, or else the 100,000 in Jerusalem will starve. So, they must accept the loss of some lives daily.

Jerusalem was the most mixed of the Palestinian cities, a crazy-quilt of Jewish and Arab communities. The Old City, with its encircling battlement walls, was almost entirely in Arab hands. So were most of the suburbs to the north, where the Arabs had cut off the magnificent Hadassah Hospital on Mount Scopus. The New City, to the west and south of ancient Jerusalem, was mainly Jewish, though interspersed with Arab pockets; the Jews also held several southern suburbs.

Outnumbered by two to one, the Jews were under severe pressure in all their positions; but by far the worst was that of the Orthodox religious community in the Old City: two thousand bookish, fragile, and mainly elderly Jews surrounded by twenty thousand heavily-armed Arabs.

On February 19 Mick wrote Emma:

This has been a sad day. I went by armored car into the holy "old city" and saw so many older Jews who were worried about their future. The Jewish quarter there is perhaps a difficult part of the city to hold. Yet by tradition, customs and heritage, it is a dear part of the Holy Land . . .

Three days later, the world was shaken by one of the worst of the violent explosions that had been rocking the Holy Land. A British Army truck crammed with dynamite was blown up on Ben-Yehuda Street in the heart of Jerusalem, killing more than one hundred Jews and shattering buildings for blocks around. Among the dead were five survivors of Nazi concentration camps—three men, an adolescent boy, and a young mother. The dynamiters were identified as British soldiers.

Mickey's fury knew no bounds. "Are these the renowned gentlemen of England?" he roared. "They act more like thieves in the night."

In a letter to his friend Nat Karr a few days later from the Negev, Mick wrote:

JUST RETURNED from the scene of the COWARDLY CRIME COMMITTED IN JERUSALEM. Gee, how we need help.

And to Emma, the first week in March:

Last night British soldiers searched a factory and confiscated their arms and left, and a half hour later, the Arabs attacked and killed eight. I shall not plague you with the details as the details have plagued me since I heard an account from one who miraculously escaped.

We understand here that the British are about to excommunicate the Jews from the family of civilized nations. What a laugh!

Mickey's bitterness against the British was hardly eased by the steady flow of Arab reinforcements into the country. On March 15 he reported to Emma:

It is frightening to watch the Arabs being armed under Treaty, and to watch the admission of the invaders: trained battalions of non-Palestinian Arabs, dressed in civil attire, fully British-armed and equipped and trained, with German and Polish officers.

It seems we are under the influence of Neutral Britain. The British manage every day to search our convoys and confiscate our arms. They have yet, to my knowledge, to hold up one Arab convoy.

London was not the only capital that was turning its back on Jerusalem in that anxious spring of 1948. President Truman, under pressure from oil-conscious generals and British-oriented State Department officials, on March 19 announced an arms embargo against "both" sides in Palestine (the Arabs had tons of British supplies) and withdrew American backing for a Jewish state.

Mickey's comment was immediate and unvarnished:

The shocking news from the USA has plunged all here into a new low. The reversal and abandonment by America will give tremendous impetus to Arab violence.

It was an hour of terrible trial for the Jews of Palestine. Somehow, for the next month or two, part of the convoys would stagger, bleeding and battered, through the Arab-irregular blockade; enough to keep the cities and settlements alive. But what would happen in mid-May, when the Jews had to face the full fury of a mass invasion?

The Army, in Mickey's view, was far from ready. It lacked organization and a staff system. Its grasp of tactical principles was not satisfactory. But most acutely, it lacked a blueprint for the training of leadership. Mickey turned to the job.

Unfortunately his arrangements for having U. S. Army manuals relayed from New York had been frustrated by a British sealing-off of underground courier channels. The British, however, could not seal off Mick's amazing memory. He locked himself in his hotel room and started writing.

Page after page flowed out in his large clear hand. Mickey's draft ranged over the entire business of war, from the breaching of barbed-wire fences to the grand strategies of encirclement.

The material was organized, of course: not under the conventional headings of Infantry, Artillery, and the like, but in line with what Mickey had decided were the special requirements of Israel's army-to-be. Nonapplicable subjects were weeded out and those of special pertinence to Palestine, such as night fighting and close-combat techniques, were liberally expanded upon. A completely original section explored the possibilities of using small task forces with armored support in the Negev and the area around Jerusalem. Mickey's goal was a pocket guide to the art of war adapted to the Haganah's special needs.

At Ben-Gurion's request, Mickey took his first chapters to Esther Bachrach, an expert typist at the Anglo-Palestinian bank in Tel-Aviv. Esther was to type them in English, for translators at General Headquarters who would be working behind Mickey turning out a Hebrew version. Soon Mick was ensconced in one of the directors' offices at the bank, rolling out more pages.

"He never stopped for an instant," Esther recalled. "I once asked him, 'Do you know this material by heart?' His answer was, 'I don't know this material. I feel it—it's in my blood.'"

The second day, Mickey told Esther to break off for lunch at whatever was her customary time: "Don't pay any attention to me." He scribbled away steadily with his left hand until nearly six o'clock, when he raced off to an appointment.

Mickey apologized for driving Esther so relentlessly. "Just between us," he explained. "I met a number of visiting field commanders yesterday and I was amazed at the gaps in their military knowledge. The Army needs these manuals the way it needs air to breathe."

After several days in which Esther Bachrach did strenuous double-duty on the manuals and her bank job, Irene Broza took over as Mick's secretary. A handsome brunette with an excellent command of both English and Hebrew, Irene had been active in Jewish Agency youth work in Europe and later confidential aide to the late Reuben Shiloah, one of Ben-Gurion's foremost behind-the-scenes lieutenants.

left: Mickey Marcus in Israel.

below: An Israeli gun emplacement guards a convoy.

I. Photos

House to house combat.

Irene found her new assignment stimulating: "He was all moods and fancies. You never knew when, in the middle of some technical discussion, he might burst into poetry or song."

Frequently work on the manuals would be interrupted by conferences and out-of-town tours; Mickey was on tap for whatever spot jobs Ben-Gurion assigned to him.

Once, returning from a field trip, he stopped in to file a report with Yakov Dori, the Chief of Staff. Dori was tied up. Mick sat down, asked Dori's secretary for a stack of paper, and went to work. By the time Dori was free, an hour later, Mick had drafted more than twenty pages on tank reconnaissance and anti-tank weapons. The disbelieving secretary reported to Dori: "This man has the energy of fifty ordinary people."

Mick's day during that period began at 6:00 A.M.—early even in a semitropical country where everybody scrambled out of bed to make the most of the cool mornings. A brisk workout on the beach with other members of the "Mahal" —the international volunteer corps of which Mick was the senior member—would be followed by a steak breakfast.

By eight Mickey had begun dictation at the Red House. At the midday lunch-and-siesta break, he would relax for half an hour at the Gat Rimmon bar; then, if his schedule permitted, take a brief nap. More often there would be an impromptu meeting in Ben-Gurion's office, during which some relatively neglected military matter would be reviewed. One such was the planning and employment of artillery units. Up to now the Haganah had no real field guns; but Mick had made his recommendations, and Ben-Gurion's purchasing agents were active in Europe. Soon after the British got out, heavy arms could be brought in. Meanwhile, Mickey organized artillery units on paper, and discussed with future field commanders the intricacies of firing tables and firing points.

Late afternoon was again devoted to the manuals.

Finally, the monumental labor of the training manuals was

all but completed: Mickey had drafted some 900 pages, then boiled them down to half that number; translated into the more compact Hebrew, his "first edition" now filled 280 closely stenciled sheets. There remained only the business of revising the chapter on Troop Movement to bring it into line with British techniques already in practice. Mickey drove up to the officers' training school late one afternoon to finish the job.

He worked steadily with Chaim Laskov, commandant of the school, for three hours after dinner. It was a warm, still evening, with an easterly desert breeze that did little to relieve the oppressive sultriness. Laskov noticed that Mick's left hand was becoming puffy from the constant writing. He proposed a brief break to tune in on the 10:00 P.M. radio concert from Jerusalem.

Mickey tilted back his chair, folded his arms behind his head, and listened blissfully to a Mozart symphony. When it ended, he remarked, "That was worth two hours of sleep, Chaim."

And he plunged back into work. Laskov, reared on the Old Testament, thought back to an earlier Warrior David who had taken delight in music. For several minutes the young officer sat drawing on his pipe in silence, watching Mickey at the bare table, scribbling away under the unshaded light. Finally the Palestinian gave voice to what was on his mind. "I don't understand."

Mickey looked up. "What—the new section on motorized movement?"

"No, no. That's perfectly clear. I mean you, Mickey." Though scarcely more than half Mickey's age, Laskov felt close enough to him to speak freely. "Why you came here, why you stay."

Mickey met his gaze soberly, but made no answer.

"I've heard a story or two," Laskov went on. "For instance —that you were offered a brigadiership in Moscow. If it was a soldier's life you wanted, you couldn't have asked for more. And I know what you left behind in the States: a beautiful wife, a comfortable home, a successful law practice . . . to join us in dust and desolation, to share our struggle."

"It's a good struggle, Chaim."

"For us it is our life. But for a man who has never been a political Zionist to throw himself into our cause—that is a tremendous thing, very heartening to a small nation abandoned by the world. It is also—for me—a puzzle. Why, Mickey?"

Mickey shrugged. "Let's just say common decency."

"But decency isn't that common today," Laskov persisted. "Forgive my curiosity, but—such a quality must have deep roots. . . ."

The American colonel shot Laskov a keen glance. He reached for the brandy bottle that Laskov kept in a handy drawer. "The truth is, Chaim," he said deadpan, pouring himself a drink, "a guy I met in Italy in 1945 told me you fellows had the strongest brandy ever distilled. I had to come over and check for myself."

Laskov gave up the chase.

Late that night, lying on his narrow Army cot, Mickey reflected on Laskov's question. Why was he in Palestine? The U.N. was involved in it, and the kinship of Jews everywhere. . . .

But Laskov was right. The heart of the answer lay deeper —and earlier. His journey toward Jerusalem had started much futher back. . . .

SIX

Mickey was born on Washington's Birthday, 1902, at 103 Hester Street, deep in New York's Lower East Side. David Daniel—his formal name—was the fifth child of Mordecai and Leah Marcus, an immigrant couple from Jassy, Rumania. His father, like thousands of other refugees from the pogroms of Europe, eked out his first living from a pushcart vegetable stand on Orchard Street, and in the evening gazed dreamily southward, where two blocks away the great girders of the Brooklyn Bridge arched across the river to that fabled borough of green fields and uncluttered streets.

Before Mickey was six, the family fortunes had improved to the point where his father, now the owner of a small stall in Washington Market, could make the triumphant crossing of the river. He transferred his brood from the dingy five-story walk-up in the crowded ghetto to an airy, cheerful apartment in Brooklyn's East New York section.

The new country was providing the hoped-for miracles: The children were in school, Leah Marcus had flour for baking her *cholleh,* and there was plenty of reason to give thanks to the Lord at the Friday evening candle-lighting ceremony.

Then, suddenly, Mordecai Marcus took ill and died. Overnight, the family's source of income was gone. They were obliged to move at once to a less agreeable street in the Brownsville district, sandwiched between railroad tracks of the Long Island line and the BMT subways. Mickey had just turned eight.

The burden of keeping the family afloat was assumed by his three elder brothers, and mainly by "Big Mike," already a stalwart at seventeen. Not only were there seven mouths to feed—Mickey's birth had been followed by that of a second sister—but with the shift from the East Side had come exposure to racial tensions.

Their new neighborhood was particularly abundant in hard-eyed young toughs who competed with each other in finding ways to abuse the "sheeny" newcomers. A favorite diversion was to close in on some aged, bookish Jew and tug savagely at his flowing beard. The tormentors soon discovered that the IRT elevated train running out to Brownsville provided them not only with plenty of victims, but with an ideal setting; once the train left its station they were free to cuff and bully the helpless old men as they liked.

It was "Big Mike" who put a stop to that. After ascertaining the routes used by the hoodlums, he led a series of raids at station stops by the huskiest Jewish youngsters he could find. The beard-pulling ceased.

It was the sort of exploit calculated to fire the enthusiasm of an already adoring youngest brother. Mickey, although not particularly brawny, was determined to follow in "Big Mike's" footsteps.

That summer, after a siege of bronchitis, Mickey was one of ten Brownsville boys offered a free two-week stay at a camp for undernourished children in Litchfield, Connecticut. His delight at getting into the open country vanished quickly. Of the five hundred boys in camp, fewer than one hundred were Jewish. The others included some of the most vicious anti-Semites Mickey had yet encountered—and several whose qualifications as "undernourished" were open to question.

Conditions at the camp are well-remembered by Noah Chase, a fellow-Brownsvillite who shared Mickey's tent:

"From the day we arrived, the Jewish segment of the camp population was under constant attack. We were roughed up by husky ringleaders whenever we dared to answer back."

If a Jewish boy held his own in a fight, there was always a bigger challenger ready to replace the first one. After a while, most of the Jewish contingent accepted the insults quietly, trading humiliation for a measure of peace.

Not Mickey. He could always be counted on to come in swinging, even if he wound up a moment later sprawled on his back. Not only did Mickey become the special target of the camp sadists, but the counselors, in the impartial manner of grown-ups, noted that the Marcus boy was embroiled in an unusual number of fights; accordingly, he was given extra doses of the standard camp punishment, castor oil.

Returning to Brownsville, bruised and wearied, Mick and Noah Chase pondered their miserable "vacation." Maybe, suggested Noah, they should have pulled in their horns like the other kids.

"Applesauce!" snapped Mickey. "My brother Mike once told me—and he got it from our father—it's no good running away. Once you start, you never stop!"

"But if the other guy is bigger—"

"What's the worst that can happen? You lose. That's better than quitting in advance."

"I dunno. I wish there was something we could do."

"There is," said Mickey, so emphatically that the other boy turned to look at him. "I'm going to build up my body. I'm going to make myself so tough that I can handle myself against anybody, anywhere."

"Big Mike" Marcus was an ardent gym fan. Somehow, in between his six-dollar-a-week job as a bookkeeper and his nightly extra stint for a paper importer, "Big Mike" always managed to slip into the Hebrew Educational Society building at Hopkinson and Sutter Avenues for a brisk session at the weights and bars, or a couple of rounds in the ring. Now he discovered he had acquired a new sparring partner.

The youngest Marcus boy dogged "Big Mike's" tracks at the gym and in the street. Always he plied his elder brother with earnest questions. It soon became evident that the little fellow's wiry body was uncommonly suited to gymnastics: He was very quickly at home among the rings and parallel bars. He was also learning to handle his fists.

Thus was cemented a relationship that had been close even before Mordecai Marcus died. Now that "Big Mike" was the mainstay of the family, his little brother idolized him more than ever. As the nine-year-old trailed his older brother all over the neighborhood, people began calling him "Little Mike." Soon they cut it down to "Mickey."

This same period saw another and very different consequence of his father's death. For a full year after the funeral, Mickey had in accordance with Orthodox Jewish tradition risen at dawn to join his brothers at the local synagogue in the mourner's *Kaddish*, or Prayer for the Dead. Gradually, as Mickey absorbed the atmosphere of the synagogue, the daily ritual had changed from a meaningless chore to a source of fascination and release. To a sensitive boy lately deprived of his father, the Voice of God held a powerful appeal.

It took little argument from Mickey's devoutly religious mother to persuade him to enroll in the synagogue's religious school or Talmud Torah, where students were instructed not only in the Old Testament but also in the Talmud.

The Talmud comprises the Jewish legal code developed

from the Five Books of Moses by the earliest rabbis, plus the elaborate commentaries added by generations of later sages. Originally handed down as a vast body of oral material, it was compiled in writing around the beginning of the sixth century A.D. to embrace seven hundred years of statute, interpretation, debate, and philosophy ranging over the entire spectrum of human behavior. It is firmly moralistic in its accent on what is right, what is wrong, and what is, under certain special conditions, acceptable.

For all of its weighty subject matter, the Talmud is an exceedingly human document, being presented in the form of lively, inquisitive dialogues salted with keen observation. It is an endless exploration of large ideas by large minds.

Day after day, upon finishing with his regular classes at P.S. 109, Mickey would hasten to the Talmud Torah to be groomed in Hebrew reading for his Bar Mitzvah, and then to be plunged into the swirling talmudic world of speculation and ancient folklore. Always the talk centered around the path of proper personal conduct through life.

Even after Mick's Bar Mitzvah at thirteen, and his increased devotion to sports, he continued to drop in at the school.

At the core of its teachings was the talmudic orientation to life, which reverenced not only God, but also the divine spirit in every individual. From this dual approach flowed a whole catalogue of precepts:

As man was small, arrogance became an absurdity, and cheerfulness a mutual obligation; a friendly smile was the least that all human beings on a lonely planet could give each other.

But as man was potentially great each person had the right to grow and fulfill himself. And the lowliest was entitled to respect: "Even the wicked are part of the handiwork of the Holy One. Observe another's honor as thy own."

Mickey's teachers were alive to the social consequences of this doctrine. A man could hardly grow in chains: therefore,

liberty was a condition of individual development. So was a
compassionate justice.

Especially binding for the talmudists, and significant in
Mickey's eyes, was the duty of the strong. Typical of the talmudic emphasis on action rather than empty ceremony was
the demand that in any social emergency, where the helm
was drifting, a vigorous hand be stretched forth to seize it:
"Where there is no man, be thou the man."

In Mickey's case, these admonitions fell upon fertile soil.
He already had before him the example of "Big Mike,"
shouldering familial responsibility in his teens. And even before his father's death, life in the Marcus household had
been rich in cooperation and sharing; now it became more so.
It was some years before the economic pinch could be eased;
meanwhile Leah Marcus walked half a mile to Belmont Avenue to save a penny on a quart of milk. It was quite natural
for Mickey, in turn, when he was given a twenty-five-cent
daily food-and-fare allowance on entering Boys' High School,
to walk the three miles each way and turn over the accumulated savings at the end of the month to his mother.

Nonetheless, life was not unpleasant on the top floor rear
at 354 Powell Street. There was constant banter among the
brothers and sisters, quick laughter, and a real sense of mutual concern, with Leah Marcus hovering gently in the background, a permissive mother who in guiding her children
toward the good life counted less on punishment than on
their natural affection for her.

Mickey had the closest thing to "favorite" status. He was
the family scholar-designate; not, as his mother told "Big
Mike" firmly, to be corrupted by "the smell of money."

There was only one flaw in this image of dutiful son and
earnest student: Mickey still got into a great many fights.
He was quick—perhaps too quick—to defend his honor with
his fists. The fact that he now generally won was small comfort at home.

There was a familial sigh of relief, therefore, when Mickey

discovered the excitement of competitive athletics—and the Boys' High coaches discovered him. The patient hours of physical training in the gym and on the playgrounds had hardened Mickey into a "130-pound ball of iron," who in his senior year suddenly blossomed forth as a crack all-around performer. He won letters in track and basketball, and as the baseball team's lefthanded first-sacker rang up the best batting average on the squad.

But football was his best sport. He was the spark plug and backfield ace of the Boys' High team.

Mick was voted best athlete in his class. His photo in the Senior Number of the Boys' High Recorder for January 1919, over the caption "as modest as a budding debutante," shows an attractive, alert-looking youngster with a smile half-ready to erupt on his lips and a tousled mop of Indian-black hair falling over his right eye. There is a boyish quality and at the same time a suggestion of inner fire.

When and where Mickey Marcus began his lifelong love affair with the U. S. Military Academy is difficult to establish. "Big Mike" has a blurry recollection of Sunday afternoons at the movies where, every time the cadets flashed by in a newsreel, Mick would point up at the screen and say quietly, "That's what I'm going to be some day." Many youngsters had such dreams; no one took him very seriously.

Timing may have been a factor. American men were fighting and dying in the war to save democracy in 1918, and Mickey's "favorite statesman" as listed in his high school yearbook was Woodrow Wilson. Also, for a boy interested in athletics, West Point was a logical goal.

But there were undoubtedly more subtle considerations. As a first-generation American, Mick shared the eagerness of his classmates to "belong." Admission to the Military Academy would be a passport enabling entry at a single leap to the most hallowed traditions of the United States. And

Army training would blend with the talmudically-nurtured impulse toward public service.

All these feelings were evidently crystallized when Mickey learned that his backfield buddy, Charlie Stevenson, had been intent on a West Point education ever since grammar school days. Charlie was a thoughtful, even-tempered boy with a fresh, open face. His father and mother both served in the Spanish-American War, the former as a company officer and the latter as a nurse; his Protestant forebears had come to America many generations before. The Stevensons lived in an old house in the Bay Ridge section of Brooklyn.

Whatever the combination of influences, Mickey now went after the prize in earnest. He got a willing hand from Dr. Arthur L. James, the Boys' High principal. His brilliant record in both sports and studies—he had been elected to the honorary scholastic society, the Arista—did not hurt. He supplemented his diploma with eighteen months of special qualifying courses at New York's City College, and in 1920 won an appointment to the Military Academy from Congressman William E. Cleary of Brooklyn.

His family was stunned. Jewish boys, and promising scholars in particular, did not make a career of soldiering. Leah Marcus wept. "Big Mike," who had been prospering in business and had set aside five thousand dollars for Mickey's education, begged his younger brother to settle for a "regular" college.

But Mick's heart was set on West Point, and he did not, his older brothers knew, either make or retract decisions lightly. So, late in June 1920, "Big Mike" and his wife drove Mickey to Manhattan and accompanied him across the West Forty-Second Street ferry to Weehawken, New Jersey. There the two brothers threw their arms around each other in an impulsive farewell. Just before the West Shore train pulled out for its trip up the Hudson, Mike reached into his pocket and took out a ten-dollar bill. "Be a good boy, Mick—and don't get into any fights!"

His schoolmates at West Point discovered he was a formidable athlete. In his junior year, Mickey fought on the varsity and smashed through the season without a defeat, coming back from a first-round knockdown in the final meet against Penn State to capture the 145-pound intercollegiate title.

In his senior year, Mickey hung up his boxing gloves and concentrated on gymnastics. His feats on the horizontal bars not only earned him another varsity "A" but an invitation to the 1924 Olympic tryouts.

Scholastically, he finished in the top third of his class, with particularly strong showings in Military Art (the study of classic campaigns) and Leadership Potential. This, coupled with his athletic record, was enough to win Mickey the offer of a Rhodes Scholarship at Oxford University in England . . . regretfully declined because of his unwillingness to leave Emma.

His career at West Point wound up in blazing triumph. Once again he demonstrated his remarkable instinct for growing. Some men have an innate impulse toward acquiring possessions; Mickey's was toward the acquisition of character.

In boyhood, he learned physical toughness; in his adolescent religious studies, he picked up the grand outlines of moral philosophy. And at West Point, again he reached out for the essence—the inspirational values and self-discipline.

Mickey emerged from the Military Academy with something more than a head full of logistics tables. He had a clear code of ethics, based on the Bible and the Declaration of Independence. He had a respect for great men and great achievements. Of all the invisible baggage that accompanied him to Israel, none was to prove more valuable than his awareness of what was most important among men and events.

SEVEN

For the Jews of Jerusalem, April of 1948 threatened to be the month of extinction. As March dragged toward a weary end, so did the last trickle of supplies to the capital. Convoys simply could not crash through; the Mufti's irregulars, swollen in numbers and confidence by Arabs from across the Transjordan border, had seized all the high ground along the access routes.

The city's water had been cut off by Arab capture of the outlying pump stations. In some Jewish suburbs, people were eating thistles and mulberry leaves.

Haganah faced a dilemma. Up to now, its policy had been to hang onto its positions while building up troops and arms. Offensive operations had been confined mainly to night forays against countryside roads and communications, and against Arab strong points in the "mixed" cities. Rarely did these attacks involve more than a company of 140 men.

Obviously no such small-unit engagements were going to dislodge the thousands of Arabs entrenched along the Jerusalem corridor.

A visiting Norwegian "expert" offered Ben-Gurion radical counsel: Dismiss the historic capital as indefensible; pull in the distant garrisons from the Galilee and the Negev; and concentrate on holding the narrow but populous coastal strip around Tel-Aviv.

The Zionist leader countered with an equally drastic but quite opposite proposal. He now had some twenty-one thousand troops mobilized. He would go over, ready or not, to the "striking fist" so urgently advocated by Mickey Marcus, and would hurl three small battalions totaling fifteen hundred men at the enemy in the Jerusalem corridor. For arms, he would allocate the entire initial overseas shipment awaited momentarily from Czechoslovakia: brand new rifles as well as some light artillery pieces, comprising nearly half the modern firepower of the Army.

The gamble was hotly debated: failure could be disastrous. Mickey agreed with Ben-Gurion. For one thing, he attached great psychological importance to the Jews' taking the offensive. For another, he had full confidence in Ben-Gurion's evaluation of the situation. If the tough little pioneer said a Jewish state without Jerusalem was unthinkable, that was good enough for the American colonel.

Two nights later, by the light of improvised flares, the first Czech rifles were landed by air on an abandoned British flying field. Within hours, the guns were in the hands of Jewish infantrymen advancing against an Arab front extending over six miles in the plains, and through two miles of rugged mountain country. "Operation Nachson"—named for the first Jew to plunge into the parted waters of the Red Sea —was launched.

It was a long and difficult struggle, in which the key height of Kastel west of Jerusalem changed hands several times. Ultimately the Haganah broke through, thereby meeting its first major test in the swingover to large-scale operations. But long before the corridor was cleared for three life-saving convoys, Mickey had been called back to Tel-Aviv by Ben-Gurion for consultation on future strategy.

High on the agenda for many months had been the military vulnerability of the Negev, whose only consistent link with the main Jewish centers was through a tiny "squadron" of Piper Cubs. Some seventeen settlements, many of them barely planted in thin sand, were literally being kept alive by widely-scattered Jewish troops who brought food through the Arab blockade, guarded pipelines, and aided in defense. How this thin network could survive the shock of an armored invasion was one of the big question marks in the Zionist position.

Mickey was no stranger to combat problems. Apart from his frontline adventures in Normandy, he had commanded field troops in the mammoth Louisiana maneuvers of 1941, and as head of the Rangers' School in Hawaii had won official commendation for his "tactical leading of troops."

And, long before he ever saw a battlefield, he had masterminded one of the most spectacular police operations in New York City's history: the 1934 raid on the Welfare Island penitentiary. The prison had been taken over by gangsters under the protection of corrupt political bosses. As Mayor La Guardia's Acting Commissioner of Correction, Mickey quietly spied out the situation, drew up sealed orders for a seventy-one-man posse, and then personally led the raiders, breaking underworld resistance.

The Negev picture was not totally unfamiliar to Mickey. In his initial surveys, he had visited the relatively accessible older communities on the northern fringes of the desert. Now a more thorough exploration was necessary. Accompanied by Shlomo Shamir, he took the rickety air journey down the coast to Kfar Darom, just above the Egyptian border and certain to be in the path of any invasion from the south.

Twice their plane was fired at from the ground as it zoomed over Arab villages, and once an air block in the fuel line forced them down briefly in the desert. But at nightfall they skidded to a landing at Kfar Darom, an Orthodox religious kibbutz which like most Negev settlements was under constant harassment from the surrounding Arabs.

Mickey questioned some of the Jewish troops. Although their morale was impressive, their information was grim. The Negev settlements, separated from each other by miles of desert, could not furnish more than thirty or forty fighting men apiece. Against Egyptian armor they could pit only barbed wire and rifles.

Mickey took a long walk with Shamir in the chilly desert night. "These Palmach boys are fine," he said. "No pretensions, no illusions. But their military position . . ." He shook his head. "We're going to have to come up with something radical."

Mickey summarized his tour for Ben-Gurion in a report that was to become a classic in Israeli military annals. "The Negev," he wrote, "will be your first theater of war. The minor war now being conducted there is for the communication lines. This will continue to be true after the invasion; the invading force will have to stick to the roads, since it will be unable to advance otherwise.

"Properly speaking, you have no military units in the Negev—merely light patrol parties. But your manpower has no equal: first-class men of mature intelligence, with the enthusiasm and dedication of real volunteers. Therefore, if you put your energies into the building of army units in the Negev you will be able to do so in a relatively short time."

Mickey's perceptive appraisal of the sabra mentality made a deep impression on Ben-Gurion. "The man understands the youth of our country better than many people who have lived here for years," he remarked to Israel Galilee, Haganah's chief political adviser. For weeks Ben-Gurion had been alternately dazzled and baffled by the brilliant but casual-mannered American colonel; he had not yet been completely convinced of Mickey's "seriousness." Now, studying Mickey's blueprint for a small mobile attacking force in the Negev —a unit uniquely designed to the Haganah's special needs and limited resources—Ben-Gurion cast aside all doubts.

"The expert who came with Shlomo," he wrote to Moshe Sharett in the United States, "has been a blessing to us. His conclusions show a marvelous grasp of the present situation, both on its good and bad sides (and the bad are neither few nor slight)."

Ben-Gurion was anxious to get Mickey's view on Haganah deployment around Jerusalem, where the patchy distribution of Jewish suburbs posed a special problem. On an earlier visit, Mickey had been appalled to discover that some of the local Haganah command regarded the broken chain of outlying settlements as an asset. "It means we are surrounded only locally," he was told. "Outside the Arab ring are more Jewish positions." Gently he had been obliged to point out that a defense line was useful only if it was continuous; without such a link between posts, the suburbs were just so many exposed positions for an alert enemy to pick off.

Now, with invasion looming by the powerful Transjordan Arab Legion, Mickey felt that some of these settlements might become deathtraps. He advised General Headquarters to evacuate any outposts "where you cannot solve the problem of supplies and communications," singling out in particular the Kfar Etzion block of kibbutzim south of Jerusalem. This was an argument he lost, Ben-Gurion clinging to his "defend-every-inch" policy. The Kfar Etzion settlements, scene of an Arab ambush in January that had wiped out a crack party of thirty-five men, were overrun by the Arab Legion in May with severe Jewish losses.

Inside Jerusalem, Mickey counseled the preparation of sharp local attacks, to be launched the moment the British pulled out, against the Arab-held districts separating Jewish areas. He felt that the side which got the jump in the early all-out fighting would gain an enormous advantage. He diagramed his ideas in quick, left-handed sketches that covered several maps with circles and arrows; three months later an article in the magazine *New Palestine* credited him with having "planned the overall Israeli strategy in the Jerusalem fighting."

The moment he saw the writing on the envelope, Mickey was alarmed. Emma's script, usually so firm and even, was spread out erratically. Mickey ripped open the envelope— and his fears were confirmed.

Mickey darling,

I hate to add to your burdens, but I am writing from my sickbed. It is two weeks since the doctor ordered me to stay home from teaching, and in that time things seem to have gotten worse. He calls it exhaustion, nervous fatigue—but labels are no help.

Can you possibly come home? The weeks have stretched into more than two months, and I find it difficult to be without you . . .

Emma's letters had been dwelling increasingly on her hopes that Mickey would be home soon, but this was the first hint of her reason. Mickey phoned down to the desk asking that he not be disturbed, and went out into the morning sunshine of the balcony to think.

Emma's illness changed everything. The wife whose love for so long had quietly upheld him, now needed him. All other priorities vanished before this one; he would have to go to her.

Conceivably he might be able to return to Palestine. In

that case, there would be no better time to break up his stay than now, in the comparative lull before invasion.

But a return trip would hinge on the speed and degree of Emma's recovery. The immediate business was to clear up whatever was on his desk and obtain space on a New York-bound plane.

His abrupt decision was received in Tel-Aviv with chagrin, not to say despair. Mickey's cheery presence and authoritative counsel had become part of the local scene. From Ben-Gurion down, a score of policymakers had come to count on him, although no single individual had an over-all picture of Mickey's activities. In the past few weeks he had spun through the valleys and settlements, sowing seeds of military wisdom whose harvest was to come at Ramleh and Beersheba and, years later, in the Sinai Desert.

Now that Mickey was about to leave, a general stocktaking occurred, and the full realization began to sink in of what the little colonel had already contributed to Haganah in his brief stay.

Yigael Yadin, acting head of the Haganah, urged Ben-Gurion to send a staff officer back with the American to increase the chances for his return. "It was vital for us to get Mickey back," he explained later. "We were trying to fight and build simultaneously. Here was an experienced soldier who knew when to hold up his hand and say 'Wait! Look!' before we got off the right path."

Other commanders were equally concerned at the prospect of losing a man whose talents had turned out to be almost miraculously shaped to their needs.

Not only was Mickey's planning responsible, as Israel's U.N. delegate Abba Eban said, for the fact that when the Arabs invaded, "Israel was ready on every front"; he was himself the cohesive element that knitted the grab-bag army of the Jews together.

Mickey was not prepared for the gloom that pervaded his

farewells. Nor did he relish the visible skepticism that greeted his earnest assurances about intending to return. Even Shlomo Shamir, his intimate in many an evening discussion, remarked bleakly, "I don't expect we shall ever see you again."

In this situation, Mickey yielded to a weakness that had plagued him since his days as a New York city official. He uttered the words he knew his listeners wanted to hear— and he trusted that he would somehow be able to deliver.

"This isn't good-by," he told the group clustered around him in Ben-Gurion's office. "When the Arabs hit, I'll be here."

Ben-Gurion eyed him gravely. "You must do as your conscience dictates, Mickey."

"It was my conscience that brought me here in the first place!"

"Whatever you decide for the future—one thing I would like you to find out. If we declare independence—are we likely to be recognized by the Government of the United States?"

"I'll track that one down for you," Mickey assured him. "It'll be number one on my agenda."

He shook hands all around. He was acutely aware of the heavy silence, the long, downcast faces.

Brave men deserved a better parting. "I'll be back," he found himself repeating impulsively from the door. "I'll be back even if I have to swim all the way!"

He flashed his reassuring grin and was gone.

Few of his listeners expected to see him again.

One or two, like Shlomo Shamir, had higher hopes. In Shamir's eyes, Mickey's decision would be a test not so much for the American as for the men and women of Jewish Palestine. Had they succeeded in impressing him with their merit and their need? Had they proven themselves worthy of still further sacrifice? Had the justice of their cause gripped an outsider so fiercely that he would have to come back?

Mickey could not at that moment have made an answer. His pledge to be on hand again when the Arabs invaded had been an emotional outburst, a commitment from the heart. Now, what to do about that earlier, stronger, even more binding commitment of the heart that awaited him in Brooklyn?

EIGHT

Two days later, Mickey was back in America. His arrival worked a miracle. Emma was pale and listless when Mickey strode into their bedroom in the early morning. By nightfall she had regained the sparkle in her eye, and the lines of anxiety creasing her forehead were all but gone. "The cure she needed," Emma's doctor told Mickey, "was you."

For a blissful forty-eight hours the Marcuses were alone, to talk and laugh and enjoy each other in the thousand ways reserved to married couples of long and close intimacy. They had a quiet dinner in New York, and wandered hand-in-hand into a Broadway movie house where the picture was far less important than the fact that they were seeing it together.

Mickey had his first moments of genuine relaxation in many weeks. Clad in an old bathrobe, he trailed Emma around the kitchen, catching up on the local gossip, teasing her about the weight she had lost during her illness.

On the subject of Palestine, he was less talkative. To Emma's query about "what it was really like over there, the day-to-day living," he replied offhandedly, "Well—sort of tense."

"There's a lot of fighting, isn't there?"

"Some. Skirmishes, mostly."

"The Hadassah newspaper is full of ambushes and raids . . . they say the Arabs are shooting at everything in sight." She looked directly at her husband. "Did you ever come under fire, Mickey?"

Mickey was suddenly terribly absorbed in studying the theatrical page of his newspaper. "Eh?" he said, "Say, look, Snippy! That wonderful Italian baritone is giving a series of concerts here starting next week! We'll have to catch him."

Emma's question went unanswered. Nor did they ever hear the baritone. The next day, inevitably, the world started closing in on them again. Mickey's brother and sisters were eager to see him; and once word of his return got around, the phone began to ring incessantly. Visitors poured across the threshold of the little frame house in Flatbush.

Emma felt a stir of uneasiness at the unfamiliarity of many of the faces, and the rough-warm accents that frequently boomed from the other end of the phone. Obviously Mickey, for all his reluctance to talk about his activities in Palestine, was still deeply bound up in them.

In a few days, Emma was back at her teaching duties. But although Mickey spoke vaguely of dropping in on his law office, he showed no signs of being in a hurry to pick up the threads of his practice. Instead, he would scan the morning papers, frowning; then put in a call to Teddy Kollek, Ben-Gurion's behind-the-scenes man at the Jewish Agency. Emma would hear terse references to tommy guns, freighters, and strange-sounding Hebraic place names.

Minutes later, Mickey would be off to some New York hotel, to be locked up in secret conference for hours at a stretch. Several times he phoned around seven in the evening, his voice weary, to say he would have to skip dinner.

One night, Emma woke at 3:00 A.M. to find herself covered with perspiration. The old fears were returning; she was going to lose Mickey.

Nonsense, she told herself. Her husband was home, safe and sound. There he was, sleeping serenely beside her.

But would he be there a week from now, or in a month?

She was not reassured by an incident that weekend in the Long Beach home of Mickey's eldest brother. The conversation over the dinner table had turned to Zionism. Suddenly, stung by some observation that he found intolerable—Emma never found out exactly what it was—Mickey leaped into the conversation with both feet. "You just don't know what you're talking about," he cried. "The Jewish state has already achieved more than enough to justify its existence—in the dignity it's restored to beaten human beings! It's taken the dispossessed and given them status as free individuals—made them their own masters, in a country where they no longer need to report to anyone. If you could see the way they live— the hardships, the deprivation—but the pride and the warmth and genuine love that flows out of every kibbutz, every last settler!"

Mickey stopped. So did the conversation. Then, a woman's voice—the wife of the man Mickey had so crushingly interrupted: "I never knew you were such a Zionist, Mickey."

"I still don't like labels. But that's one you can pin on me, if you want to."

From her husband, in soft mockery: "Mickey's been converted."

Mickey turned quickly toward the speaker. "Not converted, Fred. Educated. Palestine is a priceless experience for any man."

"Not priceless, exactly. We Jews in America have had to

pay a bill or two. Is there any appreciation of that side of it?"

Mickey stared at the man incredulously. "You, my friend, haven't begun to give the Jewish state as much as it's given you—and you probably never will. The mere existence of that state is going to free you from complexes you don't even know about. It's going to make you a better man—and a better American!"

There was no more talk of Palestine, either at Long Beach or during the drive home with Emma. But alone on his way to the garage, Mickey reflected on his outburst at dinner. It had crystallized thoughts and feelings long bubbling within him. Behind his ringing summation lay a voyage of self-discovery in Palestine.

He had gone there a non-observant Jew. In Mickey's case, the downgrading of religious observance had a certain consistency. "Religion," he once told Shlomo Shamir, "is simply a way of approaching God. Each man thinks his way will bring him closest. I've trained Irish Catholic soldiers, and I've lived among Buddhists who had no mass prayers, no church organs —just sat silently communing with the Lord. In both instances, I respected the other man's views—and he mine.

"The only people I don't respect are those who think they have an ideology which can replace God, and who in fact want only to replace God by a man who will be worshiped like a god."

Yet this was not a positive expression of Judaism; and like many of his contemporaries, Mickey was groping uncertainly for something more satisfying. In a thousand subtle ways, the fact of being Jewish penetrated his life experience. From the Hebrew-language signs over the storefronts in the neighborhood where he was born, through the street battles on the way to high school and the horrors of the Nazi death camps, the reminders had been many and constant.

Zionism, viewed from Brooklyn, did not seem to offer any

solution. Visiting a "Zionist" clubhouse in Brownsville in the 1920's, Mickey had registered sympathy—but skepticism.

Zionism experienced in Palestine, he began to realize soon after arriving in Tel-Aviv, was a different matter. For the first time, he was living in a society predominantly Jewish, where the automatic defenses born of minority status could be thrown off. The resulting sensation was exhilirating.

The awakening did not come all at once. It reached its climax on the April evening when, returning to Tel-Aviv from a reconnaissance skirmish near the walled city of Acre, he was invited to the ceremonial Friday-night supper at Irene Broza's home.

Irene's father, a European-educated banker of imposing height and bearing, did not quite know what to expect of his guest. He had heard that Colonel Marcus was little versed in Jewish tradition, and even that Mickey was "half-Irish"—a rumor traceable to the American officer's nickname, and his habit of teaming up with Irish volunteers for his off-hours boxing and drinking bouts.

Mr. Broza was startled, therefore, when at the first whiff of his wife's gefüllte fish, the visitor from America launched haltingly into Hebrew song. "It's a tune my father used to sing at Friday-night supper," Mickey explained as he groped for the words. "About how every Jew is a king on the Sabbath, and gefüllte fish is his kingly repast."

"Of course," nodded his host, smiling with deep-set gray eyes. He filled Mickey in on the words.

As the evening wore on, and the fish gave way to noodle soup, roast chicken, and a dessert of mixed stewed fruit, Mickey's memory grew more expansive. Long-buried details of familial Friday evenings on Powell Street floated to the surface.

After the tea and home-baked biscuits, Mr. Broza brought a battered Talmud to the table for his Sabbath study. Mickey wanted to know what passage he was reading.

The elderly banker translated slowly: "The man who is convinced of the rightness of his case, presses, er, with force—that is to say, the man who insists firmly on—"

"Full justice," finished up Mickey promptly, "will prevail over him who hesitates."

Irene's father shot a glance of mild reproof at his daughter: Why hadn't she told him? Irene shrugged her shapely shoulders. Who could predict anything about Mickey Marcus?

From the Talmud, the talk shifted to the Bible. Could Mr. Broza find that section, Mick inquired, where Moses sends a herald through the ranks of ancient Israel, warning off the fainthearted from the Battle of Canaan?

Mickey's host went back to his cupboard and brought an Old Testament to the table. From Deuteronomy, he translated aloud the words of Moses' crier: "Let him who is afraid and frail of spirit return to his home, so that he will not make the hearts of his brethren melt like his own."

"Moses wanted an army of volunteers," Mickey commented. "Exactly the kind Israel is forming again today." He reached out for the Bible, running his eyes over the archaic Hebrew text. "There was a truly great leader," he mused. "Moses comprehended the spirit of his army, he understood the soldier's soul."

Mickey turned to Irene Broza. "Could you get hold of an English Bible for me? I've got a lot of catching up to do."

Mickey's trail of Judaism had come full circle. Suddenly, under the warming sun of Palestine, everything clicked into place. He had a homeland, a past, a tradition—and precisely by that reinforcement, he was more free to be a creative American.

No longer, it was abruptly clear to him, would Jews have to labor under the inner burden of being a people-in-exile; a people who, no matter how much accepted, were still set subtly apart. No longer need they shuttle between the extremes of timid compliance and nervous aggressiveness. Miraculously united to a collective past, they could walk with heads high like other men.

This would not in the least, Mickey knew, impair his loyalty to the United States; on the contrary, by shoring up his spiritual underpinnings, it made him better able to serve his country.

It was natural, therefore, that a Western Jew should wish to aid Zionism. Emigration to the Holy Land was something else, involving a hundred questions of culture, climate, and personal interests. For Mickey it was not an immediate issue. He was in Palestine as an American, lending his soldierly talents where they were needed. As his onetime friend Eli Kirshner said, "He left no doubts on that score. If he loved the Negev, he let you know that it was because our desert reminded him of the great Southwest in his own country. I never met anyone so thoroughly saturated with the authentic, Jeffersonian-American outlook."

It was one of the paradoxes of Mickey's life that, pursuing his credo as an American, in the land of his forefathers he stumbled across the answer to questions that had previously eluded him.

The very intensity of this inner development complicated the problem of explaining it to Emma. The silences between Mickey and his wife, as unbearable as they were unfamiliar, grew longer. Emma would catch him looking at her, worried, out of the corner of his eye—and then turning away when he was noticed.

Early one morning a cable arrived for Mickey. His face was grim as he digested its contents. Soon afterward the phone rang. Emma heard him expostulating: "For heaven's sake, I've only been home a couple of weeks. My wife's been sick, man! You can't just walk out on someone you love!"

He was so troubled at breakfast that Emma hated to ask

him the question; but she was so upset herself that she had to.

"They want you back, don't they, Mickey."

Mickey nodded.

"What did you say?"

"I didn't say anything . . . yet." He heaved a tremendous sigh—a gesture so out of character that Emma could only stare unhappily, angry with herself for adding to his torture, angry with Mickey for having brought them both to this impasse.

That day they scarcely exchanged a word, each feeling trapped, haunted, plagued by circumstances. Emma made a sad little entry in her diary: "This is a time of indecision, dismay, and the knowledge that we are hurting each other."

Ever since Mickey's return, a standard query had been addressed repeatedly to Emma: "When's the party?"

The Marcuses had long held the reputation of the best partygivers in their circle. Their gala evenings, famous since Mickey's days as a City Hall favorite, had never needed much excuse or advance notice; and surely Mickey's homecoming was an occasion to be celebrated around the punch bowl?

Emma found herself unable to discuss the complex situation that was developing. After some ineffectual attempts at stalling, she had scheduled the expected Saturday-night gathering for Mickey's second weekend at home.

Now that date was around the corner. Emma squelched her doubts, enlisted the aid of Theodore and Dorothy Chappelle, the Negro couple who had seen her through many an earlier party, and did her best to prepare a memorable evening. When the eighteen guests assembled around her banquet table, champagne sparkled in tall, slim goblets; the fruit bowl was splendid, and the roast was succulent.

Although the goblets were of gleaming silver, the atmosphere, unfortunately, was purest lead. Somehow word had seeped through the group of Mickey's dilemma. The intended homecoming celebration, everyone now realized, might actually be a farewell. None of the toasts, banter, or nostalgic harmonizing around the glossy Steinway piano could alter that disagreeable fact.

Privately, a number of the men edged Mickey aside to question him anxiously about his plans.

Mickey avoided making a direct answer. To Reuben Levinsohn, a businessman friend, he said only: "You don't know what it's like, Rube—how helpless they are. People go out to the store to buy food, and Arab snipers pick them off . . ."

And to another friend: "Young kids and old men and pregnant women are going to be under shellfire in less than three weeks. How do you think I'll feel if I'm sitting here in this rocking chair?"

At the height of the revelry, Mickey took refuge in the kitchen. His relations with the Chappelles had always been warm. Dorothy Chappelle, slight and sensitive, remarked that Mickey looked miserable. Mick confessed that he was. He was bone-weary, emotionally drained; he would like nothing better than to stay put in Flatbush and make up for the time he and Emma had lost in the war years.

Yet how could a man quarantine himself from the fevers of the world? Mickey pulled up his right trouser leg and disclosed a scar just below the knee. That, he told Theodore, was a souvenir from Palestine.

In the living room, the party had moved away from the piano and broken up into small groups. Suddenly, inevitably, the subject in the back of everyone's mind burst out into the open.

With a delicate sense of casting, fate assigned to a man of French extraction the role of upholding the importance of love over all other considerations.

Marcel Feinier was a slender, darkly attractive man of intense, angular movements. He and his schoolteacher wife, Anne, had known the Marcuses for nearly twenty years. Holding up his hand to interrupt another discussion, Feinier made a broad gesture that embraced everything in sight— cosy living room, softly lighted porch, and chattering guests —and pronounced firm judgment: "This is where Mickey belongs. Right here with his beautiful wife in his lovely home. Here and no place else."

Up from the couch scrambled Walter Soderstrom, another close friend. "Now, wait a minute, Marcy. That's for Mickey to decide. It's not such a simple problem."

"And I say it is simple!"

The buzz of other conversation subsided.

"A man has a good wife," Feinier went on. "They love each other very much. They should be together."

"Granted. But—"

"It's Mickey's obligation to stay home."

Several women nodded. Soderstrom shook his massive, blond-thatched head. "What about his obligation to a cause he believes in? And to good, honest people who are counting on him, who need him?"

"Emma needs him more."

"Who are you to say, Marcy? Have you seen the situation in Palestine?"

"No—and neither have you."

"But I've heard Mickey talk about it. Something new is being born in the Holy Land. A man can't turn his back on history, Marcy!"

"And I say he can't turn his back on his wife. If you were a really loyal friend, you wouldn't even be arguing about it!"

Soderstrom advanced and shook a plump finger in Feinier's face. His cheeks, normally pink, were flushed a bright red. "You watch your tongue, Marcy! When it comes to—"

Reuben Levinsohn pushed between the disputants.

"Round one, round one," he said gaily. But the tension did not ease.

Feinier, eased into a chair by his wife, continued to shoot off sparks: "It's easy for Walter to talk about idealism and glory. But Emma's the one who'll be left alone if something happens—if Mickey should—"

He never finished the sentence. Emma had just walked into the room.

After that, the party broke up. By unspoken agreement, the formalities were raced through quickly; couples shuffled toward the door, with Marcy Feinier and Walter Soderstrom keeping stiffly out of each other's way.

In fifteen minutes, the last of the guests had gone. Emma and Mickey stood facing each other on the porch, alone. Mickey shook his head. "I should have kept an eye on Marcy. He gets so steamed up about the people he loves."

"I'm glad somebody does." She stepped ahead of him into the house.

"Snippy!" The pain in Mickey's voice cut into her heart. But Emma could hold back no longer. She wheeled around. "Don't you think people can read, Mickey? Don't you think they can put together the stories you tell—the shortage of food in Palestine, the blockades, the air raids that they won't be able to stop? What does all that mean for your chances, Mickey? If you go back, it can't be just as an observer. How long can you keep dodging the snipers and the land mines, once the whole country is a battlefield?"

"That's not the point, Snippy. The issues are bigger than any one man's safety!"

"Or any one woman's happiness." Bitterly, Emma started up the stairs.

Mickey ran after her and grasped her hand. "Please, Snippy. I haven't said I'm going. I couldn't, with you feeling this way. Let's think about it, talk about it some more . . ."

Armored cars on the Jerusalem front.

Convoy on the way to Jerusalem.

I. S. I.

He gestured toward the silent, breeze-stirred street. "It's a nice night for a walk . . ."

Emma felt her knees trembling. "No, Mickey. I'm too tired."

"Then do you mind if I do? I won't be long."

Emma continued up the stairs. Mickey would be back, after walking off his tensions. But would he be back if, once again, he flew halfway around the world?

She tried to force the question from her mind, but it would not go. Mickey had very personal ideas about death. He did not recoil from it as the ultimate horror, to be avoided at all costs. Returning to the Army in the face of the Nazi threat in 1940, he had explained: "One has to live like a man—and die like a man." When Grace Cantelmo, a much-loved friend of theirs, succumbed to illness at thirty-five, Mickey had held up to his grieving wife two books: a slim volume of Keats, and a dictionary.

"How do you judge a book?" he demanded. "By its bulk —or its contents? A human life should be evaluated in the same way."

Emma removed her earrings and dropped them on the dresser. Her eye fell on an old picture of Mickey in cadet uniform: freshly-scrubbed, firm-chinned, eyes shining with knightly zeal.

"No wonder I fell for him," she thought to herself, repeating a long-standing joke. "It was that uniform."

But it wasn't the uniform, and never had been—not even on that distant evening when she trudged through the snow-filled streets to her first "real" party, at the home of her cousin, Bob Hertzenberg. The party was for various collegians home for the Christmas holidays. When flu laid low several female guests, Bob had hastily drafted his "kid cousin" Emma—and hoped nobody would notice she was of high school age.

These hopes were dashed by his first view of the fill-in guest. Emma's simple, fluffy schoolgirl frock was in glaring contrast to the low-cut gowns on display. The high piling of her thick black hair, in a pathetic attempt at worldliness, merely accented her tender years. There was terror in her eyes.

Of course, if one really looked, Emma was rather pretty, in a childlike way: clear brow, neatly spaced features, rounded chin . . . But who would look?

Emma stood squeezed just inside the door, trying to melt into the wall. A Gershwin ballad floated up from a portable phonograph on the floor. Several couples stumbled past her, and a crew-clipped youth daringly waved a pocket flask in her direction. Emma looked away. She wished she were home doing French verbs.

At the other end of the room, grandly sampling the punch as befitted the guest of honor, stood Mickey Marcus with his host. Mickey was resplendent in tight-fitting gray dress uniform, the black braid plastered in manly bars across his ample chest.

Mickey's eye caught someone in the shadows near the door—someone shy and frightened, with long, graceful legs and high cheekbones. He nudged Bob Hertzenberg lightly. "Who's that?"

Bob peered across the room. "The redhead in the green dress? That's Natalie Fischer. She goes to—"

"No, no. That one."

"Barbara? Say, she's—"

Mick shook his head. Without putting down his cup, he thrust a powerful arm around Bob's waist and lifted 150 pounds of startled youth off the floor, depositing him again in a position where he unmistakably faced Emma.

"That one."

"Oh, her? That's my cousin Emma. She's just a kid,

Mickey. A fill-in. You'll have more fun with Barbara Simon. She knocked 'em dead at Princeton last month—"

"I want to meet Emma."

Bob shrugged. "Oh, well. It's your party. . . ."

Mickey danced with more self-assurance than technical skill. Emma was no more tense than most high school girls would have been in similar circumstances: that is, she managed to propel her legs mechanically while her upper body was frozen rigid.

"Relax," Mickey told her good-humoredly.

"Don't give me orders, Mr. Marcus. You're not on your parade grounds, you know."

"I know. And I'm very glad of it."

He looked full into her face. Emma was tall and slender—almost his height—with startling bright hazel eyes of a liveliness to match his own. She met his gaze for a moment, then looked away, blushing.

"You seem awfully confident," she said.

Mickey grinned. "We're trained to be leaders of men."

"But not women. That's a different technique."

"Hey." Mickey stopped dancing a moment. "Kind of snippy, aren't you . . . I think that's what I'll call you— 'Snippy.' Do you mind?"

Emma flashed a smile that turned his heart over. "How can I argue with a leader of men?"

Mickey never did get to meet Barbara Simon, the belle of Flatbush and the conqueror of Princeton.

Emma went to her first cadet hop later that year—and missed very few thereafter. Her courtship had all the traditional elements of a West Point romance: wispy organdy, delicate corsages, and squadrons of gallant young men—plus a few variations that were purely Mickey.

Stationed on Governor's Island after graduation, Mickey became proud owner with Charlie Stevenson of a fourth-hand Dodge touring car that could be entered only by climbing over its jammed doors. The sight of Emma negotiating this barrier provided much merriment.

Emma's parents, however, were not amused. Her mother had considered Emma rather too young to attend Mickey's graduation hop without a chaperone, and certainly too young to undertake housekeeping in Puerto Rico—Mickey's next post if he stayed in the Army. Her father, a prosperous real-estate dealer, was frankly dubious about the earning prospects of a second lieutenant.

And so, in 1927, they were married. In the interim Mickey had put in three years at night law school in Brooklyn, and resigned his Army commission. The joint income of the newlyweds was something under $150 a month, most of it from Emma's salary as a fledgling teacher.

Mickey was working as a law clerk. While awaiting his admission to the bar, the couple stayed with Emma's parents in Flatbush. As soon as they had saved a little money, they scrambled into a tiny three-room apartment on Ocean Avenue. Although the furniture consisted largely of orange crates, they insisted on doing their own furnishing, when and as income permitted.

With his first sizable fee, Mickey raced out and made a down payment on a Steinway grand piano—so large that it eliminated further problems as far as the living room was concerned; there was no space for anything else. To Emma's halfhearted protest that this did not meet the issue of a dining-room table, Mickey replied, "Man does not live by bread alone." He knew how important music was to Emma. It was a gesture she could never forget.

Although the Steinway was purchased for Emma, it opened new vistas of delight for Mickey. Listening to his bride as she played and sang after dinner, he found himself transported into the world of music. He began tuning in regularly on the Saturday afternoon opera broadcasts. Then, with Emma as his musical guide, he made his first visit to the Metropolitan Opera House.

Soon there were some forty librettos piled up in a corner of the Marcus bedroom, and Mickey—with no formal training in music—was lecturing to a fascinated Emma on the structural elements in operatic composition. It was a passion that never left him.

Meanwhile, via civil service examination, Mickey had entered governmental legal service, moving from the Treasury Department into the U. S. Attorney's office, where one of his colleagues was Thomas E. Dewey. He also plunged into Brooklyn politics, aligning himself typically with the underdog Republican organization and winning leadership of the party club in the Second Assembly District.

Several evenings a week, while Emma entertained teacher friends, Mickey devoted himself to fund-raising projects for such institutions as the Hebrew Educational Alliance. Sundays were set aside for making the family rounds: first, Emma's parents, and then the various Marcus households.

For all of these preoccupations, Mickey was an extraordinarily thoughtful husband, quick with the little attentions dear to the female heart. He never failed to notice what Emma was wearing, and his admiration was never silent.

Surprises flowed from him: silver trays picked up at auction, a hand-carved music stand, an odd piece of jewelry. Always it would be something that Emma had, in an off-guard moment, admired. Wifelike, she would protest Mickey's extravagance—while secretly delighting in it.

In 1934, Mayor Fiorello La Guardia waved his wand over Mickey, appointing him Deputy Commissioner of Correction, and the five "golden years" of Emma's marriage began. The Marcuses moved for the third time, into an old apartment house on East Nineteenth Street with a king-size living room. Their joint earnings were now substantial, and they could afford to entertain a great deal.

Emma was constantly being amazed by the number and variety of people who counted Mickey among their dearest intimates—sometimes on brief acquaintance. Such different personalities as Shlomo Shamir; Mayor William O'Dwyer of New York; Brigadier General Julius Klein of the Jewish War Veterans; prize-fight manager Joe Gould; and Czar Dyer of Michigan, a West Point classmate who hadn't seen Mickey in years, all referred to him as "one of my closest friends." Major General Thomas H. Green, former Judge Advocate General of the Army, describing many chats with Mickey, said: "I came to admire and respect this man. I felt rather close to him."

Emma was not quite prepared in 1940 for Mickey's decision to go back into uniform. At thirty-eight, her husband had just come into his own in the City administration with formal appointment to the Commissionership of Correction. A great favorite of La Guardia, he had prospects for political advancement as bright as those of any man in the country.

But Mickey had been following events in Europe and coming to his own conclusions. Hitler was going to force the United States into war. As a West Pointer, Mickey had been trained for exactly this kind of situation; it was the basis for the government's investment of time and money in him. Fortunately, he had long ago taken a commission in the Reserve and kept up with it via correspondence courses.

In vain Emma argued that Mickey was not of draft age, that as a major city official he was excusable from call-up to active duty, that his contemporaries were not rushing off to arms at the first blast of the bugle. No one pointed it out at the time, but John Adams, Jefferson, Jay, and Hamilton all gave up brilliant law careers to join the American Revolution; and Mickey Marcus of West Point was very much a spiritual child of 1776.

Emma could still feel the bleak chill of the fall day when Mickey departed from Grand Central Station for his National Guard camp in Alabama. Mickey had tried to muster up some of the old gaiety: "You'll be coming down for Christmas before you know it, Snippy. We'll build a snowman in the cotton fields." But she sensed even then what Mickey confided in a whisper to Murray Gurfein, one of the old friends who pushed through the ring of reporters and cameramen for a final word: "This is it, Murray—the beginning of a long and terrible time. Once I get onto this track, I'll never get off it—not for the rest of my life."

Her intuition—and Mickey's—had not been wrong. For seven long years, she had lived on letters, hopes, the excitement of brief reunions—and the torment of suspense. Even with the end of the war, her marriage had not regained its balance. Hitler was dead; but his ghost hovered over her life and Mickey's, as over the lives of so many millions.

She was one woman. She had been a faithful wife, a good daughter, a conscientious citizen. All she asked for now was to have at her side the husband she loved.

Was that too much?

The question spun around and around in her head—like an endlessly revolving wheel that refused to stop.

NINE

Mickey's footsteps echoed through the silent streets.

Like Emma, he looked back upon a long road of laughter and passion and companionship. But since 1934 he had also been pursuing a parallel path—one of increasing involvement with the world at large—on which the first towering landmark had been Fiorello La Guardia.

When a fed-up New York citizenry swept La Guardia into office, Mickey was appointed First Deputy Commissioner of Correction. He had worked hard for La Guardia's candidacy, but only as a matter of conviction; he wanted to help boot the crooked politicians out before going into private law practice.

Suddenly he was in municipal government, and in it up to his ears, taking charge of the spectacular raid on Welfare Island. That story, reported in headlines throughout the country, started the new reform administration off with a bang.

La Guardia and Mickey clicked from the first. The ex-

World War I flyer, who liked to be addressed as "Major," had more than a military background in common with his West Point protegé. Both men were stocky, intense, and belligerently honest. Both spoke their minds freely—and in almost the same shrill, clear voice.

Mickey had a broad field for operations. After his cleanup of the city's prison system, he was ready to launch a constructive program. Mickey turned to the Talmud on his desk.

"At the time of his birth," said the sages, "man is not created by nature to be the author of either good or bad works. He must be trained."

This gave special importance, Mickey felt, to first offenders. He brought into the prison system its first full-time psychiatrist, to conduct examinations and make recommendations regarding paroles.

Mickey's friend Ed Cantelmo recalled dropping in with the Deputy Commissioner one day at the House of Detention for Women in Greenwich Village. Mickey stopped first in the kitchen to satisfy himself that the prisoners' menu was adequate by Health Department standards, then toured the place.

"On every floor," reported Cantelmo, "he spoke to new arrivals in the friendliest fashion imaginable. He was especially pleased to report to a girl interested in music that he had succeeded in getting a piano for her."

The mayor began consulting Mickey on a variety of matters. In 1936 La Guardia appointed Mickey a Temporary Magistrate to help relieve pressure in the congested Manhattan courts.

That summer, Mickey teamed up with Tom Dewey in an unusual operation. Closing in on the Lucky Luciano vice ring, Dewey had the problem of how to protect from Luciano's hatchet men the one hundred-odd underworld informants who were his chief witnesses. Mickey locked them up under special guard; an instance of "extraordinary cooperation," said Dewey, "without which the case would not have been brought to a successful conclusion."

It was now an open secret that La Guardia planned some sort of advancement for Mickey; a news story in the summer of 1939 described the Deputy Commissioner as "one of the mayor's closest advisers." A judgeship was reported in the works, or candidacy for district attorney of Brooklyn.

Instead, when the promotion came in April of 1940, it was to leadership of the department he had been running unofficially for years. Mickey's salary, as Commissioner of Correction, was nearly doubled, to $11,000 annually.

With a completely free hand, he pushed for a program that would be regarded as farseeing even in the 1960's. Rather than spend $2,000,000 on a new Raymond Street jail, he argued successfully for allocation of the money to parks, playgrounds, schools, and hospitals: "If we clear our slums, give our boys more recreational facilities and better schools, eventually the need for penal institutions might disappear."

Juvenile crime remained his greatest concern. Young lawbreakers, he felt, could be rehabilitated—but not alongside "hardened felons whose very presence seems to contaminate the boys." He urged the establishment of work-and-study communities "far out in the country" where juveniles could be taught a trade while gradually brought into personal adjustment with society.

La Guardia, like Emma, was startled by Mickey's announcement that he was going back into uniform. The mayor was in no strong position to protest, having done much the same thing himself when he left Congress to become a flyer in 1917. And he was doubly understanding of how a Jewish soldier would feel about the Nazis.

"It's got nothing to do with my being a Jew," snapped Mickey. "I've always thought of myself as an American—an American who happens to be of the Jewish faith. I'd feel the same way about Hitler if he was pushing Buddhists around, or Seventh-Day Adventists. An attack on any religion is an attack on all of them."

When Mickey went South in 1940 with his federally activated National Guard unit, it was as a Lieutenant Colonel and Judge Advocate of the 27th Infantry Division. His first Reserve commission, granted when he resigned from the Regular Army in 1926, had been in the Field Artillery. He had been persuaded in 1939, on the strength of his considerable legal experience, to shift to the Judge Advocate General's Department.

The Division commander was Major General William N. Haskell. He appointed Mickey his Headquarters Commandant; and although a Judge Advocate is not normally allowed to command troops in the field, Haskell obtained special authorization from the Pentagon for Mickey to lead the division's Special Troops in the 1941 summer maneuvers. Commanding a picked force of several hundred infantrymen, MP's, signalmen, and an ordnance company in sham battle through the Louisiana swamps, Mickey made such a spectacular showing that Haskell recommended him for promotion to full colonel as a "very virile executive, an all-around able and forceful commander."

In November 1941, General Haskell took Mickey along on a countrywide tour of divisional training bases. They were in Seattle, Washington, when news broke of Pearl Harbor.

Mickey declined a Pentagon assignment and hurried to join his division, already being shifted westward to Fort Ord, California. Late in March, Mickey flew into the Pacific to join his unit.

The 27th Division was assigned to defend the outer ring of the eight islands comprising Hawaii. Its new commander, Brigadier General Ralph McT. Pennell, was military governor of the island of Hawaii. Mickey was his Executive

Officer, handling under martial law everything from traffic violations to price control, dealing with a fantastically mixed population of Hawaiians, Caucasians, Japanese, Filipinos, Chinese, and Koreans.

Within four months General Pennell recommended Mickey's promotion, saying: "His outstanding performance has enabled me to give my attention to my primary duty, the protection of this island."

In November 1942, the Division was transferred to Oahu, the populous inner island famous for Honolulu, Waikiki Beach, and Pearl Harbor. The new commander, Major General Ralph C. Smith, assigned Mickey to organize and command a Rangers' Training School designed to prepare troops for the rigors of jungle warfare. The eight-week course, to be taken by two hundred men at a time, involved toughening exercises; guerrilla tactics and hand-to-hand fighting, including judo; and special instruction in camouflage and survival.

Mickey trained some eight thousand men. Later, operating as regimental combat teams at Makin and Kwajalein, and in divisional strength during the landings at Saipan, the Rangers earned a reputation for tough resourcefulness rivaled only by that of the British commandos—a reputation jealously guarded to this day.

Mickey had hoped somehow to work his way loose from staff status and obtain a field command with his Rangers. Instead, he found himself pounced on in the spring of 1943 by General Hilldring to bolster the Pentagon's overburdened Civil Affairs Division. The move to the General Staff in Washington had its brighter sides: reunion, at least for the summer, with Emma; and promotion to full colonel.

Much of Mickey's new activity was in the top-secret category. One clammy summer evening, in the apartment the Marcuses had temporarily rented in the capital, Mickey lingered long over the scribbled yellow pages that were his nightly "homework." Around midnight he shoved back his chair, stood up, and suggested a walk.

Emma waited while Mickey got his brief case, carefully locked the yellow sheets inside, then stuffed the brief case under lock and key into a closet.

"Something important?" she asked.

"The Italian surrender terms—if they're okayed."

Emma smiled. "I'll bet."

She should have known better. They were the Italian surrender terms, drawn up under special assignment from General Hilldring; and they were followed by Mickey's draft of unconditional surrender for Germany.

In the round of historic interallied conferences that began in 1943, Mickey was consistently among the American advisers. He traveled first to Cairo in November, for the Roosevelt-Churchill-Chiang Kai-shek meeting.

Before continuing on to the Big Three session at Teheran, he was taken in General Marshall's personal plane for a quick glimpse—his first—of Palestine. Back to Emma came a stack of photographs, a topaz necklace, and the observation, "This has been the most absorbing month since I entered the Army as a plebe."

At Teheran, he was struck by Stalin's comprehensive grasp of the military situation. "He never turned to his advisers for information. He seemed to have it all in his head. He made his own decisions and he made them fast—without bothering to be tactful."

After Teheran came Dumbarton Oaks, where the U.S.-British alliance, in separate meetings with the Russians and the Chinese, laid the foundations for the United Nations. From his conference quarters, Mickey wrote to Emma:

It is fascinating to watch the different national traits of the delegates: the youth, absolute confidence and definite convictions of the Russians, in contrast to the vague broad prin-

*ciples of the British. But we have the plan. And we are so very
willing to compromise.*

A few weeks later, at the Roosevelt-Churchill conference
in Quebec, Mickey once more sat at the elbows of the giants.

When the Big Three met at Yalta in February 1945, as the
Allied armies advanced on Berlin, again the stocky colonel
with his brief case hovered in the background.

By now his experience was such that Hilldring felt no
surprise when General Clay requested Mick's transfer to his
Occupation staff in Germany. On the eve of Mickey's departure in May, General Hilldring pinned on his chest the Distinguished Service Medal. The lengthy citation noted Mickey's "firsthand experience" gained in Normandy, and his role
in the "negotiation and drafting of the Italian Surrender
Instrument, the Instrument of Unconditional Surrender of
Germany, and the international machinery to be used for the
control of Germany after her total defeat."

The plane carrying Mickey to his new post landed in
southern Germany early in May, a few days after the liberation of Dachau. Under General Clay's standing instructions,
the first order of business for newly arrived senior officers
was a visit to the still-smoldering concentration camp, the
most terrible of the Nazi prisons which was devoted exclu-
sively to mass murder. Clay wanted his top people to see
"exactly what the Nazis had done."

With a young lieutenant from Texas as his guide, Mickey
made the prescribed rounds. He stood in stunned silence
before mountains of grotesquely flung bodies; stepped disbelievingly into gas chambers whose walls were still scrawled
with the names of the dying; stared into a cavernous oven,
and felt his skin creep as the lieutenant translated the neatly
lettered sign above it: "Please wash your hands after you
work; cleanliness is next to godliness."

After an hour's relentless tour the lieutenant, seeing the strained features of the older man, suggested they call a halt. Mickey shook his head. He had to see everything, burn it into his mind beyond forgetting.

At last the nightmare was over. So, for the moment, was Mickey's faith in God and man.

How could the human spirit be so defiled—and for the "crime" of cherishing an ancient faith, of clinging to observances that were dear to his own mother? What Heifetz lay unrealized in that tangled heap, what Spinoza? Was this the climax to man's progress on earth, the final destiny for the "immortal being of infinite worth" shaped in the image of God?

Mickey went behind a barracks building and wept.

Two days later, speeding through the moonlit countryside with a tank column conducting clean-up operations farther east in Germany, Mickey heard a ragged, eerie chorus of voices from the nearby woods. He asked the driver of his jeep to turn off.

In a clearing, awaiting transport, they found a group of some fifty liberated Jewish prisoners, "gray skeletons with hollow faces eaten away from inside and out," standing at attention and singing. Mickey recognized the song: the Hatikvah, the traditional Jewish song of the hoped-for return to freedom in Zion. They were singing with the enthusiasm of a people who had returned from the depths of hell to the land of the living.

That encounter made a deep impression on Mickey. To his rage over Dachau was added the conviction that everything possible had to be done to aid the pitiable survivors; "the door to Palestine must be kept open."

With full encouragement from Generals Clay and Patton, Mickey worked furiously to make conditions tolerable for the stranded DP's. His letters reflected his bitterness against the Nazis. Hatred, so rare in Mickey, for once was stirred. He wrote to George Medalie:

Sir, standing on the earth where once stood a Berlin, I experienced a joy that rioted within me.
I am a firm believer in non-fraternization. Personally, I have the greatest difficulty in remaining civil to any German. I have seen their "KULTUR."

Always, the plight of the refugees was with him. En route with General Clay to Munich, he scribbled his impressions for Emma:

What catches your eye and makes you slacken your pace and think of Emma Lazarus' poem inscribed on the Statue of Liberty is the mass of DP's wandering about—lost—a body of humanity that no one seems to want . . . no haven to go to, no friends. All of this is depressing and fills one with sorrow. Will the sadness ever end?

Mickey's Army job in Germany was important. He was officially right-hand man to the late Major General Oliver P. Echols of the Army Air Force, who was in turn Deputy to the often absent General Clay. As Executive for Internal Affairs of the U. S. Group Control Council, then its Acting Chief of Staff, and finally U. S. Secretary-General in occupied Berlin, Mickey was in effect the number three man in making American policy—a role exercised mainly in lengthy after-hours discussions with his two superiors.

The talk ranged over many topics—Clay recalls Mickey as a "delightful conversationalist"—but it always came back to the business at hand: How much reconstruction was desirable for Germany, and in what direction?

Mickey, curiously enough, held no brief for trampling the Germans ruthlessly underfoot. His personal resentments were one thing; his responsibilities as an official entrusted with the protection of American interests were something else.

Long before, in Washington, he had taken the basic stand that German militarism should be annihilated, but not the country. At a White House conference, he had strongly supported the War Department's arguments against Harry Hopkins, who favored the drastic "Morgenthau Plan," by which Germany would be reduced to a vast farmland.

Now, even after Dachau, Mickey still saw the main German danger as the military tradition. This would have to be uprooted, along with the Nazis who had so skillfully exploited it, and replaced by a long, thorough education in democratic processes.

But the Germans would ultimately have to run their own country, and be allowed sufficient industry to support themselves. Otherwise, they would be a permanent drain on the economy of the United States, and a certain source of future trouble.

This was essentially the Washington-approved doctrine under which Clay was operating—self-government to be restored as quickly as possible, beginning with food distribution and transport at the local level. In this initial phase of the change-over, involving the reorganization of city administrations, Mickey was particularly active. Clay and Echols were acquainted only with Federal government structure; Mickey's "knowledge of municipal government and the operation of police forces," said Echols in one of numerous commendations, "made his services invaluable."

At the Potsdam Conference, this time attached to President Truman's staff, Mickey got his third close-up view of Churchill and Stalin. He also attended a meeting of the three top Western generals—Eisenhower, Montgomery, and Koenig—with Marshal Zhukov, and concluded that "soldiers handle problems with more equity and speed than the boys with the striped trousers and high hats."

Weighty ideas now preoccupied Mickey. In a letter to Emma he wrote: "We are the only force on earth for high moral purpose. This must be the end to all wars. With the present powerful weapons of destruction, we must think in terms of the entire globe."

In the fall of 1945 Mickey was awarded the Bronze Star and Army Commendation Ribbon for "splendid leadership" and "unusual ability to deal with international problems." The Legion of Merit, for which his name was submitted three times, was withheld on various technicalities, all of which, in the words of General Echols, "seemed very flimsy to me."

At the turn of the year, General Hilldring wrote to General Clay asking if he "might possibly be willing" to part with Mickey: "I have an important assignment for him and would rest much easier at night if I knew he was on the job."

The assignment was to take over the mammoth task of selecting hundreds of judges, prosecutors, and lawyers for the trials of major war criminals at Nuremberg and in the Far East. Clay reluctantly agreed, and Mickey returned to the Pentagon as head of its War Crimes Division.

There were a few treasured days with Emma in Washington before he was off again on a ten-thousand-mile whirl around the map. He attended the trials at Nuremberg long enough to assure himself that at the very least, the Nazi way of life would be "thoroughly exposed for future generations to brood upon"; then he headed for home, ready at last to hang up his Army jacket for keeps.

Six months later came the visit by Shlomo Shamir, and Mickey's introduction to the trials and the promise of Palestine. There he had seen a living alternative to the death mask of Dachau . . . an alternative consistent with John Adams' view of the American mission as "the emancipation of the slavish part of mankind."

Mickey turned onto the elm-lined fragrance of Westminster Road and started home. An ancient and powerful phrase rang in his ears: "Where there is no man, be thou the man."

If the need exists, and you are qualified, it is your duty to serve.

The deadlock was finally broken by direct intervention from Tel-Aviv. Spokesman for Ben-Gurion was his ranking representative in America, the supple-minded, soft-voiced Moshe Sharett, whose black mop and trim diplomatic mustache were to provide a field day for caricaturists when he later became Prime Minister of Israel.

Toward the end of April, Sharett asked Mickey and Emma to join him and his wife for Passover lunch in a midtown Manhattan restaurant. Mickey as usual dominated the proceedings, chatting through the meal. Sharett, a gentle and erudite man with a command of fourteen languages, had little to say; he sat gazing thoughtfully at Emma.

Afterward, the couples went for a stroll in the spring sunshine through Bryant Park. Mickey paired off with Mrs. Sharett, leaving his wife with the Palestinian diplomat.

Sharett guided Emma to a quiet bench near the fountain, and fixed his large, brooding eyes on her. "You're very happy to have Mickey home."

Emma turned defensively. "Is that so unnatural?"

"Not at all. Your husband is a most extraordinary man. I can appreciate what it must have meant to you, every time you let him out of sight."

An intensity came into Emma's voice. "Can you, Mr. Sharett? Can you, really?"

"Mrs. Marcus . . . I do not pretend to be all-knowing. But I have lived, I have raised a family. I have some idea of what you must have endured during Mickey's long absences."

"Yet you want to take him away from me again."

Sharett did not answer at once. " 'Take him away' sounds so harsh," he said finally.

"It is harsh, Mr. Sharett."

"Could we say 'borrow'?" Sharett took a deep breath. "I

wish I could convey to you how important Mickey has been in remaking Haganah . . . as teacher, friend, guide. With him around, our young officers had someone they could turn to, someone whose judgment they could rely on with complete confidence. One could almost say, Mickey is the pillar on which the new Haganah is based."

Emma sat silently for a moment, watching a group of youngsters dance in and out of the spray of the fountain. When she spoke, it was in a small, choked voice: "And what do you think my life is based on?" Emma felt her self-control slipping; she reached into her handbag. "Why must it be Mickey, Mickey, always Mickey? For seven years of war, all I had was glimpses of my husband: a meeting here, a weekend there. The people of Berlin saw Mickey, and the Hawaiians, and every Army base on the map—but all I had was a collection of postmarks! Do you know how it feels to teach children all day and come home to an empty room at night?"

The Palestinian nodded his sympathy. "Ordinarily it would be impossible to make further demands on you."

"Then how can you—"

"Because this is not an ordinary situation. I don't speak only for Mr. Ben-Gurion—or even for our half-million settlers. Perhaps they could face the loss of decades of back-breaking effort; they have suffered before." Sharett paused. "But, what of the refugees at our gates? For them there is nothing left but a vision, a dream. . . ."

Emma wrenched her glance away. "I know, I know. . . ."

"Perhaps you do not know, completely, just how desperate our situation is. We dare not admit it publicly; our morale at home might disintegrate."

Emma's eyes came back to the grave, compassionate face. "Is it . . . hopeless?"

"No. Never that—thanks largely to what Mickey has already accomplished."

Emma felt a sense of panic, of a battle lost. "You shouldn't put me in this position! It's unfair!"

"Unfair, yes," agreed Sharett. "Unreasonable, too. Even heartless, if you will. And yet—necessary."

"There must be someone else—" the words were wrung out of her—"somebody, somewhere!"

"Perhaps there is. But I haven't been able to find him."

Emma was silent. She looked down the path toward the Public Library, along which Mickey and Mrs. Sharett were returning, deep in conversation.

"It comes down to this," said Sharett. "We cannot yet give our boys the arms they require. We cannot even clothe them properly for the field. If we have been able to find the leadership they need—can we deny them that, too?"

Two hours later, Emma sat alone in her bedroom. Mickey was downstairs, going through the evening papers. Emma knew she could hold Mickey back, but it would be like clipping an eagle's wings; what remained would be some sort of a creature, but no longer an eagle.

The notion of choice was an illusion, really; there was no choice. Once you loved a man, you wanted him to fulfill himself, not to be consumed by doubts and regrets. If Mickey's heart was set on going, he might as well be sent on his way freely, with her blessing.

Emma got up and started toward the hall.

Mickey did not say much when she told him. But from the expression of relief that flooded his face, she knew she had done the right thing—the only possible thing. Ten minutes after he left for the Jewish Agency, she collapsed on her bed, too worn out for weeping.

On April 30, Mickey and Emma had a farewell dinner at the home of Dr. Emanuel Neumann, the veteran Zionist leader. Two days later, Mickey stood in the doorway of the plane that would take him on his thirteenth journey away from the United States. From the observation deck, a dazed Emma looked after him, trying to fight off the premonition that suddenly stabbed at her heart.

Mickey saw the shadow that crossed her face. "Chin up, Snippy!" he called out. "I promise you, I'll be back in June!"

It was a promise tragically to be kept.

TEN

The twin-engined Dakota, piloted by a Haganah volunteer from South Africa, zoomed diagonally across the eastern Mediterranean. At the Greek islands, it veered sharply left and headed for the coast of Palestine. Because Lydda Airport was now in Arab hands, the plane set down on a landing strip near Tel-Aviv.

Mickey Marcus was back on Zionist soil.

Within half an hour Mickey had climbed the winding stone staircase to Ben-Gurion's office, and was poking his head through the anteroom door. "*Shalom*," he said softly.

The girl sergeant, busy at the typewriter, acknowledged the greeting absently—then whirled her head around to look again.

"Mickey!" she screamed. "Mickey Stone!"

A messenger, on his way through Ben-Gurion's door, stopped and stared. So did a bronzed officer thumbing through a filing cabinet at the door.

Moments later Mickey was surrounded by a babble of excited, disbelieving voices: "Mickey, is it really you?" "You came back to us—from America?" "It's impossible. Such things don't happen."

Mickey frowned. "I told you I'd be back. Aren't you used to seeing a man keep his word?"

There was a heavy silence. The officer stepped forward. "Forgive us, Mickey. We have become too skeptical. After all, we know what lies ahead; and we never thought a man in his right mind, a man who has everything in his own country, would come back to us . . . after seeing for himself how poor our prospects are.

"You must realize, your coming here in the first place was for us a pretty big thing. 'He must be mad,' a lot of people said. Now you're back—and I believe you really are mad. But here we are all mad—and you are one of us." He held out his hand. "Welcome back, Colonel."

Mickey squeezed the officer's hand between his powerful paws. "Thank you, Dan . . . is the Boss in?"

Several people sprang to open the door of Ben-Gurion's office.

Mickey advanced to greet the rugged little figure seated behind a mountain of papers on the desk. "*Shalom*, Boss. I won't tie you up long. But I've got word you've been waiting for."

The famous brown eyes glinted piercingly. "Yes?"

"If you hold the borders in the north till May 15, and then declare a Jewish state—it will be recognized by America."

"How do you know, Mickey?"

"I've sounded out a few people in Washington. I think you can count on my prediction."

Ben-Gurion looked out through the curtainless window onto the sparkling whitecaps of the Mediterranean. A distant sail shimmered on the horizon. " 'As cold waters to a thirsty soul,' " he said finally, " 'so is good news from a far country.' "

Mickey went downstairs to the Haganah Operations room
in the basement, where a battery of Intelligence officers filled
him in on developments during his absence. There was en-
couraging news from the north; Haifa had been occupied by
the Jews, despite calculated assistance to the Arabs by the
departing British. In the eastern half of the Galilee, spectacular charges by Jewish forces had captured Tiberias and
driven the Arabs out of long-beleaguered Safed.

In the south, the picture was less comforting. The Negev
was being steadily infiltrated by irregulars of Egypt's fanatic
Moslem Brotherhood.

And the center remained troublesome. After the Haganah's
capture of Kastel, the jagged peak where a Roman fort had
once dominated the approaches to Jerusalem, three major
convoys were pushed through to the capital. On April 20,
however, the Jews had been forced to withdraw for regrouping
in the south, and the Arab noose had promptly tightened
again. In spite of local successes inside Jerusalem, the lifeline
to the city was therefore once more imperiled.

At 4:30 P.M. on May 14, 1948—surrounded by enemies,
worn down by siege and hunger, unequipped for modern
warfare, and virtually friendless among the nations—the democratic State of Israel proudly proclaimed its independence.
David Ben-Gurion, as Prime Minister and Minister of Defense in the provisional government, announced that the new
republic would be "based on the principles of liberty, justice,
and peace as conceived by the prophets of Israel."

The dead land of the Dead Sea had blossomed into life
again.

The wild dream of European visionaries led by Theodore
Herzl had been hewn into reality by the strong arms of
latter-day pioneers. Reversing twenty centuries of passive acceptance, the Jews were standing up to make their own fate.
No longer would they be everywhere a vulnerable minority

to be destroyed piecemeal; in Israel, at least, future men of ungenerous spirit would have to face a united nation.

Two-thousand years of pent-up frustration erupted in the streets. Middle-aged refugees, spirited sabra beauties, and chubby schoolboys joined hands in wild dancing of the hora; venerable doctors and even bearded Orthodox scholars cast off the inhibitions of dignity to laugh and cry and throw their arms around each other.

This was deliverance at last—deliverance almost beyond belief for those who had survived pogroms and slaughter; a homecoming and a welcoming embrace, after an eternity of wandering across an inhospitable earth.

It set off a spontaneous emotional outpouring to which the most sophisticated observer could not remain immune.

Ben-Gurion had scarcely pronounced the name of the re-born state when Cairo's Spitfires were raining bombs on defenseless Tel-Aviv. Huge new Egyptian tanks crunched over the bony soil of the Negev. Armored legions from Transjordan and Iraq swarmed across Palestine's frontiers from the east, ringing the Holy City with fire. And the Syrians joined the Lebanese to strike with renewed fury in the north. On five fronts the Arab-Israeli war was joined, locking in mortal combat two closely related peoples who for centuries had shared the gently poetic salutation, "Sha-lom—Peace."

For the Zionists, exulting in the attainment of their age-old dream, melodrama was piled upon drama: American recognition came at once, as Mickey had forecast.

But the celebration could not be prolonged. A multitude as of locusts was descending upon the hosts of Israel. The moment of liberation might be the moment of final doom. And indeed, as captured enemy timetables later revealed, the Arabs expected to be in Haifa by May 20, and in Tel-Aviv and Jerusalem by the twenty-fifth.

They had reason for their confidence. Against a Jewish

force of hastily trained amateurs who had been under steady combat pressure for more than five months, they were putting into the field five completely fresh professional armies with overwhelming superiority in weapons, and especially in such normally decisive equipment as air power, armor, and artillery.

Mickey, surveying the picture in an all-night conference on May 14-15 with Ben-Gurion and Yigael Yadin (now officially head of Haganah), summed matters up: "Well, there it is, Boss—what we have and what we haven't. Since there's nobody else and nothing more we can depend on—all we can do is fight!"

To Mickey, standing before a map in the Haganah Operations room and weighing the massive Arab superiority in striking power, the indicated enemy strategy was obvious: a crushing body blow at the frail Israeli center that would snap the Jewish state in half and score a quick knockout.

As Mickey saw it, the only real hope of the Jews was to maintain their lifeline to the west—the ports of Haifa and Tel-Aviv—through which, if they could hang on elsewhere long enough, supplies might ultimately arrive that would enable them to reverse the tide. An Arab slice-through to the coast would dissipate that hope by quickly bringing the ports within range of the enemy's big guns.

There was no doubt in Mickey's mind about what would be the best operational plan for the Arabs. The question was whether the invaders had the unanimity of goals and the unity of command necessary to achieve it. Here, if Haganah calculations were correct, was the hidden element that made the Jewish position merely desperate rather than absolutely impossible.

The "united Arab" banner was riddled with mistrust, mainly revolving around the ambitions of King Abdullah, the British-installed puppet who ruled the Bedouin wasteland of Transjordan. Abdullah wanted Jerusalem as a matter of international prestige. And, for a nucleus in building a family empire that would ultimately embrace Syria and Lebanon, he wanted as much as he could swallow of the rest of Palestine.

This directly clashed with the plans of the Grand Mufti of Jerusalem, who saw himself as the center of a Jerusalem-based empire. But it was no great comfort to the other members of the Arab League.

The Syrians naturally eyed Abdullah warily; they were as much interested in frustrating his designs as in grabbing for themselves the headwaters of the Jordan.

Egypt, intent on maintaining its leadership of the Arab League, could hardly relish advancing the cause of a prospective rival.

Iraq was concerned primarily with acquiring the oil refineries of Haifa; Lebanon, with upholding its uneasy status as a country 51 per cent Christian; and Saudia Arabia was not involved at all.

The divergence in Arab goals would not, however, slow down the Centurion tanks crashing into the Negev, or dampen the powder of the Arab Legion shells pouring into Jerusalem; at best, it might win a reprieve from immediate annihilation.

Mickey's main hope lay in Abdullah's fascination with Jerusalem. The American colonel knew that the Legion's armor would be least effective in the narrow alleyways of the old capital. As Mickey said to a close friend in New York, "If they'll just waste enough time trying to capture Jerusalem to let us get our supplies in through the ports, once we get our heavy stuff we'll kick the devil out of them on the central front."

Within thirty-six hours, the invasion pattern emerged: Or rather, what emerged was the absence of a clearly defined pattern. Although the Israeli defenses shuddered under a barrage of blows at no less than eight places, the Arab Legion was being deployed in and around Jerusalem. This was bad news for the long-suffering inhabitants of Jerusalem; but from the strictly military viewpoint, it gave the Israelis an important breather. Now the Haganah might be able to organize a front-by-front defense. Mickey would have his fighting chance.

Word from the Negev soon made it clear that it would be no more than a fighting chance. Waves of Egyptians were pouring across the flat, hard desert floor: ten thousand men spearheaded by twenty tanks, forty armored cars, and fifteen hundred other vehicles, and accompanied by two full battalions of heavy artillery. The Negev, laced with British-built roads, and far too vast to be covered with defenses, was custom-made terrain for armor.

Overhead, unopposed Spitfire fighter-bombers blasted a path for the invaders.

Against this modern force were pitted twenty-seven scattered settlements "fortified" with barbed wire and defended by thirty to one hundred and twenty riflemen apiece.

The Egyptian attack was in two columns: a main, armor-weighted drive straight up the coast toward Tel-Aviv, and a truck-borne infantry thrust about a third of the way down the border, designed to team up with Moslem Brotherhood irregulars already in the Negev for an advance toward Hebron.

The northward plunging Egyptian column met no immediate opposition, since Arab villages were sprinkled in its path directly above the frontier. The first battle came at Kfar Darom, which stood two hundred yards east of the highway. Here the Egyptians hurled eight tanks on May 15 against the small garrison, but were somehow beaten off. They detached a small infantry-artillery group to keep the settlement under fire, and the main body of invaders continued up the coast, their heavy guns booming.

More shattering to the Negev defenders than the enemy

shells themselves was their impact on morale. To a barefoot guerrilla whose own most violent explosive was a hand grenade, the thunder of giant cannon was understandably disheartening. Sweating settlers looked up in frustration as new Spitfires, their R.A.F. insignia still gleaming, swooped low to demolish irreplaceable water towers.

To compound the crisis for the Israelis, an urgent radio message arrived at General Headquarters in Tel-Aviv from the north: Syrian armor had ripped a hole in Jewish defenses below Lake Tiberias, opening up the possibility of ploughing through to Arab-held territory in the central Galilee.

One group in Haganah favored abandoning the overrun Negev to concentrate on the north and center. They wanted to take a stand against the Egyptians only below Tel-Aviv, where the bulk of the southern Haganah forces were deployed.

Mickey earnestly disagreed. "The Egyptians must be checked at once," he told Ben-Gurion. "Theirs is the best-equipped army and the most dangerous line of advance." He advocated a bold assault upon Gaza, a main Arab base of eighty thousand population some twenty miles up from the Egyptian border, "to break the spearhead of the Egyptian drive."

If this was too daring for General Headquarters' taste—and Mick perceived at once it was—he insisted that in any case the Israelis had to counterattack at once, rather than leave the initiative with the enemy.

"You'll say we haven't the forces to attack. I say we have. Even with light units we can raid the enemy's military centers before he's had time to get organized—stop him from placing his guns and preparing his armor. We can exploit his fear of night-fighting, jab at his supply lines, keep him off balance. That's the way the American Rangers were trained to fight: to maintain a strategic defensive against superior forces, by constant, harassing local attacks!"

Ben-Gurion, remembering Mickey's report on the Negev which had envisaged just such an aggressive defense, nodded. He agreed to review with the American a shipment of new weapons just unloaded at Haifa, and to allocate at least some to the Negev; he would send Mickey south with them in the hope of holding the battered Negev together.

ELEVEN

The invaders' momentum had to be checked.

Available for the job, with Ben-Gurion's blessing, were a batch of radio-equipped jeeps and modern machine guns freshly received from the United States and Czechoslovakia. Used together, they offered a combination of firepower, mobility, and communications not previously within reach of the Israelis. In the absence of real armor, they might serve as a kind of junior tank group capable of slashing hit-and-run attack, around which a Negev defense line at once flexible and aggressive could be established.

Such at least was Mickey's confident theory. He was delegated by General Headquarters to supervise its execution on the spot.

Formal command of the new unit was entrusted to Israel Carmi, a beefy, blunt-spoken veteran of World War II campaigns in Libya, Italy, and Yugoslavia; a commando-fighter

May 10, 1951. Emma Marcus holds ribbon of Israeli Order of Independence presented to her by Premier David Ben Gurion at West Point memorial ceremonies.

Homeward bound: in a plain casket of rubbed white pine, the body of "Brigadier Stone" is taken from Jerusalem museum for transport to Tel Aviv and the United States.

July 1, 1948. The funeral of Colonel David Marcus.

both by training and temperament. Carmi's orders from Yigael Yadin wasted no words: "Organize an assault force within 48 hours and go down to the Negev."

At Tel Hashomer camp outside Tel-Aviv, where the Officers' Training Course was being conducted, Carmi recruited his company and platoon commanders and assembled his motorized group. Backbone of the outfit was two jeep companies of fifteen vehicles apiece. Each jeep carried a pair of sturdy, accurate machine guns: a medium Czech Beza mounted on the front right, and a light, German-made Spando .34 on the left rear.

In addition, Carmi had a company of Palmach infantry carried on half-tracks; a company of Israeli-made armored cars; a support company equipped with six three-inch mortars and six medium machine guns; and a platoon of sappers. Soon afterward his firepower was buttressed by artillery pieces: two long-barreled 20 mm. Piat anti-aircraft guns which at Mickey's suggestion were placed on half-tracks and converted to anti-tank weapons.

For his section commanders, Carmi selected outstanding volunteers from the Haganah's "Gadna" or youth battalions: boys of sixteen to eighteen who had received premilitary training in school. His jeep drivers had in most instances handled similar vehicles before in the British Army. Qualitatively, his seven-hundred-man force left nothing to be desired.

By the end of the day, one jeep company was ready to move. Carmi ordered it to proceed south at once. Mickey decided to accompany this advance formation; Carmi would follow later.

The jeeps spun onto the road and headed south, all lights cut because they would be threading through enemy-held areas. Under an orange-slice moon, they moved at a forty-mile-per-hour clip past grain fields and groves of eucalyptus, making a wide circle to avoid the Arab village of Mesmiya.

The party traveled at battle-ready, with no covering on the vehicles. The men's sleeping bags were slung over the hoods, creating from the distance a rounded, bulky effect that baffled —and apparently frightened—enemy spotters; Arab intelligence reports that later fell into Haganah hands described the jeep column as "light modern tanks, of Russian make."

By dawn the company reached the Negev entry post of Negba, a dry and dusty settlement of some 220 souls. The kibbutz sat on a gently curved plain, planted with a scattering of willows, acacia, and olive trees whose necessity as shade-makers was only too clear. Already, as the sun swung over the eastern hills, mouths were parched and arms hit the air against the gnats.

The jeeps were camouflaged and dispersed through the settlement, sometimes with blankets strung between them to provide shade; the men would try to rest through the day in preparation for continuing southward through the enemy lines at nightfall.

Guard posts were being assigned to the communications trenches running through the settlement when a distant droning throbbed in the air. Against the pale blue sky to the west, two tiny dots appeared—only a fraction of the Egyptian air strength, but a fraction capable of wreaking havoc on shelterless ground troops without a single anti-aircraft gun. Negba was already the twice-daily target of raiding planes based just across the border in Egypt.

At the company commander's signal, most of the men leaped into the four-foot bunkers constructed by the settlement dwellers. Others, however, stood as if paralyzed while the two dots, now recognizable Spitfires, drew nearer and lower, the five-hundred-pound bombs under each wing in plain sight. At two hundred feet, they loosed their bomb-loads. One thudded harmlessly into a barren hillside; the other demolished a small outbuilding.

Mickey joined the company commander under a stripling

willow. "They'll be back to dive," he whispered urgently. "Tell your boys to open up with their rifles. Use your fire-power!"

The Spitfires wheeled and thundered in for the ground kill, strafing the exposed company at close-up fifty-foot range. The roar of their engines, and the ping of machine-gun bullets running a stitch along the trenches, at first drowned out the C.O.'s shouted commands. But as he and Mickey seized tommy guns and fired at the diving Spitfires, others followed suit, creating a massed volley. The Egyptian pilots, bullets rattling off their fuselages, climbed up and out of sight.

The Israelis had several wounded. Shock was widespread; few of the troops had ever before been under air attack.

But already there was a partial return of confidence from the realization that even lowly rifle fire, properly concentrated, could drive off the terrible Spitfires.

Mickey passed among the soldiers, slapping backs, making jokes, exchanging a quiet word. He paused before a youngster who had been nicked twice in the forearm: "You keep this up, Gershon, and the Egyptians won't have any bullets left."

Another boy, pale and trembling from shock, found himself smiling as Mickey scooped a gnat out of the air and addressed the insect fondly: "I remember you, Waldo, from my last visit."

This was the kind of thing the Palmach appreciated. The American colonel, in case there had been any doubts about it, was no mere staff adviser writing memos in a Tel-Aviv office, but a soldier who kept his head—and his courage— under fire.

As a husky sixteen-year-old said to his platoon commander, "That man gobbles up a fight with all ten fingers."

The penetration into the Negev could not continue until after sundown, when Egyptian planes ceased their surveillance of the roads. Soon after dark the jeep company set out for the inland settlement of Dorot, temporary headquarters of the Negev Brigade. Again they moved without lights and followed a roundabout route; although Arab villages were fewer in the south, the Israelis might soon be crossing the Egyptian lines.

The precaution proved well-taken. At 3:00 A.M. Mickey's radio intercepted an Arabic-language conversation in the hard, dry accents of Cairo.

"What's happened to your advance, Captain? You're supposed to be protecting my flank!"

"Impossible. The road is full of mines. We can't move before morning."

To the listening Israelis, it was clear what lay behind this exchange: the Egyptian reluctance to do battle at night.

Before dawn, Mickey was at the scrub-and-cactus approaches to Dorot, a cluster of primitive wooden buildings surrounded by deep wadis (river valleys) and low, rolling hills. He entered the headquarters shack to find Nahum Sareig, chief of the Negev Brigade, sagging red-eyed over a stack of maps and organization charts.

Sareig had just been knocked out of his elaborate headquarters at Niram nearer the coast by an Egyptian air raid that demolished his refueling installations and wrecked half a dozen vehicles. He was trying to piece together the elements of his eight-hundred-man command in this crowded hut.

It was obvious that the youthful Palmach commander, after his long trials in the double assignment of fighting and keeping open the Negev supply lines, was crushed to find himself in a totally new kind of war for which he had neither the equipment nor the training. Sareig's dejection, Mickey discovered, extended down the line of command and was even more severe among the troops. These boys had withstood siege, cold, and hunger bravely. They had fought rifle-slinging marauders with their bare hands; they could not be expected to do the same thing against tanks and Spitfires.

The "Wild Beasts of the Negev," famed for their unconquerable spirit, were in a crisis of morale—stunned and
baffled by the blinding power of the enemy.

Mickey's first step was to show them the new weapons of
the jeep company, surpassing the total previous firepower
of the Israelis in the Negev. Sareig's veterans, shuffling around
the jeeps in their sandals and patched-up work shoes, mut-
tered their envious surprise at the fine uniforms of the newcomers—and their delight at the sturdy Bezas and Spandos.
They were still fingering the guns when Carmi rolled up
with the remainder of the raiding force.

Now spirits were visibly, if faintly, lifted. With such reinforcements, new plans could be drawn up. Carmi's officers
followed Sareig's staff men into the headquarters shack and
plunged into heated conference.

Mickey sat in a corner, following the discussion intently.
At first the Israelis talked in English, out of deference to
their American adviser; but inevitably, in the excitement of
debate, some lapsed into Hebrew.

Mickey could see that the argument was spinning in circles:
whether the jeeps should be used to bolster the weakest settlements, or the main strategic centers? Or would it perhaps be
better to spread them out across an arbitrary east-west defense
line?

Mickey asked for the floor. His proposal was simple and
direct: "You must attack."

One of Sareig's staff officers made an impatient gesture of
dismissal. Mickey pretended not to notice.

"I know you think you're weak. But if you concentrate
everything you've got—the jeeps, the guns, all your infantry
—you can put together a striking force that'll hurt!" Mickey
leaped up from his chair. "You've got to stop playing around
with small groups. Gather everything into a single force—
and strike!" He crashed his left fist into his palm.

The dissenting officer greeted this with a sour smile. "Let

him talk," he remarked in Hebrew to his colleagues. "He thinks he's going to teach us about desert fighting."

Mickey could not follow the man's words, but the tone was unmistakable. He addressed himself to the officer directly. "Do you understand what your assignment from headquarters is? To throw back the Egyptian attack. You'll never do that by merely returning the enemy's fire. You must knock him sideways, keep him off balance. In your situation, the word 'defense' is fatal. Let's erase it from the Negev dictionary!"

This forceful statement, so totally at odds with the previous discussion, left the Palmach men breathless. Mickey turned to Carmi.

"You must explain to them, Carmi. The fighter who starts out on the defensive is lost in advance. Initiative itself is half the battle. You must hit and hit and hit again, until it is the enemy who begins to have doubts, who starts thinking defensively. When you've achieved that—when his morale begins to slide—you are close to victory."

Carmi translated rapidly, putting his whole two-hundred-pound frame into the argument. After a spirited exchange in which most of the company joined, he reported back to Mickey: "They want to know where you would direct such an attack."

"At Gaza."

"Gaza?" There was a howl of dismay. "But that's the biggest Egyptian base in the Negev!"

"Exactly. By capturing it you will cut off their army farther north, leave it without supplies, and prevent other units from spreading east."

Sareig spoke up. "But there's a huge garrison in Gaza. We've never been able to get even a patrol into the city."

"A patrol isn't the same thing as an offensive operation. You've got to stop paying out your resources in small change.

You people want to prod with your finger, when you have the capacity to strike with your fist!"

Still the worried headshakings continued. Without the need for every objection to be translated for him, Mickey saw that here, as at headquarters in Tel-Aviv, his plan against Gaza was too bold for acceptance. To him, it seemed transparently clear that Gaza was the heart of the Egyptian position, and that a lightning night thrust against its surprised garrison would be successful. But the Palmach boys were not trained in taking the grand view or in organizing co-ordinated actions: and they were still absorbing the impact of the shattering Egyptian firepower.

He would have to settle for less. The important thing, after all, was to get the "Wild Beasts" back on their fighting feet, to restore the cocky drive that had been their greatest asset. If he could only strike a spark somewhere, get them to start thinking aggressively. . . .

Even as he was groping for a new approach, a young company commander came over to him hesitantly. "You want to—throw spikes into the Egyptian advance. Is that the idea, Colonel?"

"Spikes, nails, monkey wrenches—now you're talking! Here you have an enemy who hates to fight at night; whose communication lines are getting longer as he moves up the coast; whose bases are within striking distance. Are you going to let him parade scot free right into Tel-Aviv and Jerusalem? Or are you going to chop him up—pin down his troops—disorganize his offensive?"

Now, there were some thoughtful nods. Imperceptibly, the mood of the discussion had shifted. There was no further mention of a slash at Gaza, but other plans were being put forward—small plans, calculated to harass rather than paralyze—but plans for attack nonetheless.

From a hillslope near Beit Hanun, northeast of Gaza, an Arab gun battery had been mercilessly shelling Niram, the former headquarters settlement. A quick night strike, it was decided, could put the battery out of action.

Mickey was delighted. Rubbing his hands, he reviewed approvingly the plan drawn up by Sareig and Carmi. A company of jeeps would loop south and west to deliver heavy diversionary fire at Gaza; meanwhile Palmach infantry would circle northward to make a sudden surprise lunge at the gun battery.

"It's a beginning," Mickey told Carmi. "After a success or two, your boys won't be so bothered by material inferiority. You know what Napoleon said about fighting bigger armies: 'I concentrate my troops and rout one flank. That causes confusion. Then I attack somewhere else—always with all the forces at my disposal.'"

At sundown, the jeeps were wheeled out of their hiding places, refueled, and assembled in convoy formation. Mickey jumped into his former seat in the lead car.

Carmi placed a brawny hand on his shoulder. "Nothing doing. Headquarters warned me about you."

"But I've got to see how the boys handle themselves under fire," Mickey protested. "And the reaction of the garrison in Gaza."

"The main thing you've got to do, according to my orders from the Old Man, is stay alive. There's a long war ahead."

Reluctantly, Mickey joined Nachum Sareig in a staff car that would wait at a rendezvous point between the two attack areas.

The jeep company, with Carmi in command, set out for the kibbutz of Beeroth Yitzchak below Gaza. The infantry marched in the opposite direction, seeking such sparse cover as was available while they watched for the muzzle flashes that would betray the location of the Arab gun battery.

Shortly after midnight, the jeeps rolled up a dirt road from Beeroth Yitzchak toward Gaza, taking up a semicircular position about a hundred yards from the edge of the darkened town. At Carmi's signal, the entire company opened up with all arms: Bezas, Spandos, and tommy guns—a hail of concentrated fire that lighted up the cracked floor and loess-yellowed rocks of the desert.

For several minutes there was no response from the town: only a hubbub of shouts, curses, and general confusion. Finally the Egyptian garrison swung into action, spraying the area south of the town with wild but prolific artillery fire. Since the Israelis had essentially accomplished the purpose of their feint, they shifted formation, fired a few more bursts, and withdrew.

The infantry meanwhile had been creeping up on the Arab-held hill. At the height of the jeep attack four miles to the southwest, they opened fire from a distance of fifty yards.

The Arab gunners were taken completely by surprise. In the darkness, they had no idea whether the many-angled spurts of fire came from a force of twenty men or two thousand. Most of them did not stay to find out. They scrambled to their feet and ran.

The Israelis found a half-dozen abandoned field pieces. Having little previous acquaintance with artillery, they were unable either to fit the guns onto their carriage wheels or to drag them away without wheels; so they settled for destroying the breeches and the firing mechanisms.

Now the Egyptians in Gaza belatedly spotted the all-but-completed action on the hilltop. They opened long-range artillery fire, but did not venture forth into the uncertainties of the night.

Carmi's force was first to link up with Mickey and Sareig. "The citizens of Gaza are not musical," the burly commander reported. "They don't appreciate the sound of shooting—our shooting."

"You've hit the enemy," said Mickey, "but mercifully. You've only snapped his head back." He turned to Sareig. "You see, Nachum, the Egyptian now faces you with a bloody nose. He can still take the ring—but he doesn't feel quite so sharp! Now let's see how your 'Wild Beasts' made out."

Approaching the meeting point, Mickey heard the subdued chant of male voices in the exultant "Song of the Palmach:"

> The eagle's path is in the sky lanes
> The wild ass climbs along his mountain trail;
> Our path is wherever we meet the foe . . .

Mickey turned to Sareig: "They did all right, Nachum!" The returning men were loaded with booty, excitement— and, for the first time in many days—confidence. "Look at these Brens!" crowed a dust-caked young redhead. Everybody was talking at once, describing the details of the action and showing off the material captured: Bren guns, rifles, and submachine guns.

More important than the booty, in Mickey's view, was the extraordinary change in morale. These men were winners. They had bearded the fearsome enemy and sent him sprawling. Perhaps the invaders were not so unconquerable after all.

Mickey clapped one of the boys on the back. "Were the Gyppos frightened?"

"And how! They scooted over the hill like rabbits."

"Next time don't let them get away. Taking prisoners cuts down their manpower—and they already have more guns than gunners."

The next morning, Mickey led a careful review of the operation. "That's the way we have to keep hitting," he summed up—"against bigger and bigger objectives."

There was less disposition to argue with him now, but a hard core of doubters remained. Raiding a gun post was one thing; taking on a concentration of armored vehicles would be something else.

"Everything in war is a gamble!" Mickey told them. "If you wait for the perfect situation, you'll never move. You have to act with what you've got!"

"And we haven't seen the last of those Spitfires," he was reminded gloomily.

"That's for sure. But that, too, can be converted into an asset. The Egyptians put too much faith in their British equipment. When you show them that even their Sunday punch can be opposed by rifles, they're going to be shaken! Every bullet can bring down a plane—if you hit the gas tank or engine or pilot."

There was a snort of protest. "You're asking for quite a bull's-eye!"

"David did it with a slingshot, didn't he?"

Appreciative grins greeted his response—to fade abruptly at an unmistakable hum in the distance. For a split second, the hutful of officers listened. Then they picked up their personal arms and scrambled for the half-sheltered command trench outside the shack. Other trenches were similarly filling up with troops carrying rifles and tommy guns.

Only one man broke the pattern—a jeep company officer who had left his uncamouflaged vehicle near the staff hut. Disregarding Mickey's warning, he ran toward the car and was hit in the leg by a machine-gun burst from the first of three Spitfires zeroing in on the camp.

Elsewhere, however, the line of rifles in the trenches was spitting back steadily at the fighter-bombers.

The Spitfires swept low over the headquarters area, emptying their machine-gun belts in vicious, raking fire. But they did not return for the customary second diving run. Instead, they loosed a spate of small bombs from a relatively high altitude. One crashed through a dairy shed; another exploded some fifty feet from the command hut.

The returning staff officers found the hut in sorry shape. The far wall had been caved in by the blast, and the building was riddled with bullets. On the table where Mickey had been sitting a few minutes before, an ugly stitch bit into the wood. In the corner, his canvas bag was pierced with holes.

The raid left its usual aftermath of depression among the Israelis. Comrades had been wounded and buildings splintered. The victory of the night before no longer seemed so splendid.

Mickey sensed the returning frustration, and the ebbing of that aggressive spirit on which he knew success depended. He unzipped his bag and dumped out its contents.

"Hey, look at this hat!" He held up a much-ventilated khaki "tembell" or 'fool's hat" of the settlements, and plopped it on his head. "I'll march through Tel-Aviv with this and be hailed as a war hero!"

Next he picked up a shirt and, grabbing a knife from the table, sliced off its bullet-punctured sleeves. "Very nice of the Gyppos—now I've got a summer shirt!" Encouraged by several smiles, Mickey went outside to the clothesline where he had hung a pair of freshly washed khaki trousers that morning. The trousers too sported several bullet holes in the leg. He cut them off ceremoniously at the knee. "Now my summer outfit is complete!"

The men laughed, not so much in amusement as in the reassurance provided by Mickey's presence. Confidence flowed out of him from an apparently bottomless reservoir, enveloping everyone in sight. Perhaps, as Mickey said, the raid had not been so devastating after all: "What did their bombs hit, for all that waste of gas and ammo? A few planks!" If the American colonel could remain so stalwart in their cause, could they do less?

At this delicate juncture in Negev morale, Haganah General Headquarters in Tel-Aviv came through with the next best thing to a squadron of fighting planes: an assignment to offensive action. Yigael Yadin was becoming increasingly worried by the secondary Egyptian column slashing northeast across the desert. If this force succeeded in linking up with Arab Legion detachments around Hebron, a combined assault could be launched from the south against Jerusalem.

Carmi's raiders were ordered to cut the road leading up from Beersheba in the Negev to Hebron. Pinpointed as their target was a bridge spanning a wadi near the Arab village of Dhahiriya, about halfway between the two cities.

This kind of operation—a disruptive thrust deep into the heart of the enemy territory—was exactly what Mickey had been urging. He let out a whoop of enthusiasm, grabbed the bewildered Carmi around the waist, and lifted him off his feet. Then, while all available explosives were being rounded up from the Negev settlements, he sat down with brigade staff officers to plot the demolition raid.

It was decided to send a company of fifteen jeeps led by Carmi, accompanied by three command cars carrying sappers, two hundred pounds of T.N.T., and the wooden supports that would be necessary to hold this relatively small charge in place under the bridge. One platoon of five jeeps would be deployed to cover the approaches from Beersheba; a second would take up positions opposite the nearby Arab village; and the third would guard the demolition engineers while they raced against time.

Although the objective was almost due east from Dorot, the raiders planned to mislead enemy intelligence by making a wide flanking movement southwards, describing a huge "U" before reaching the bridge.

Toward sunset Mickey reviewed the route laid out by Carmi, and inspected the troops who would make the long, dangerous sweep behind enemy lines. "You'll pull it off," he assured them. "You know the smell of victory."

The forecast proved accurate. The bridge was blasted into the riverbed in a neatly timed operation that required the use of only a single bullet, against a donkey-mounted Arab rifleman who wandered onto the scene. And on their way back, seeking to evade Egyptian air patrols, the jeeps met the test of bucking across treacherous sand dunes.

Mickey was elated. "Now you're cooking with gas!" he told the brigade staff. "The Egyptians will have to post guards at all bridges—that means drawing troops from the line.

"Their gunners are already losing sleep at night—scared of another Beit Hanun. Even the ones who escaped there will be spreading stories—puffing up the size of the action— creating panic and doubt and all the little misgivings that take the heart out of an army.

"Keep smashing at them—give them no rest! Don't split up your forces, don't get bogged down in detail. They'll go on being afraid as long as you go on attacking!"

From that day, a new pattern of campaign developed in the Negev: attack, occupy, attack elsewhere. Egyptian supply lines were ripped apart; munition dumps set afire; railroad tracks dismantled. No post was secure against night attack, never twice from the same direction. Soon thirty jeeps and a few hundred men were controlling a vast area of desert theoretically occupied by thousands of powerfully armed Egyptians.

As Carmi and Sareig stabbed relentlessly at the rear of the lumbering enemy, Mickey's words rang in their ears:

"Don't worry about the individual settlements; you can't help them with an extra dozen men. Your job is to wear down the enemy, defend the Negev as a whole.

"Remember, you now have striking power! And you're facing soldiers who aren't really interested in the outcome, who want only to get home unhurt; while your boys want to fight. Do you realize how important that is? They want to fight!"

Mickey himself concentrated on keeping that fighting spirit high. Slipping out from under Carmi's watchful eye, he went out on several reconnaissance patrols. A Palmach veteran testified that "with a brace of machine guns, he threw a hell of a scare into a whole company of the Moslem Brotherhood."

The American officer visited settlements and dropped down from the skies into isolated Palmach camps. Betsall Amiv, then a junior officer in the desert, recalls Mickey stepping nonchalantly out of a pancake-landed Piper Cub to deliver a quick, concise lecture on the employment of jeeps in modern warfare . . . a subject on which a British military writer credits Mickey with revolutionizing Israeli military thought.

Summoned back to Tel-Aviv the last week in May, Mickey bounced into the office of Israel Galilee, the Haganah political chief. Bronzed and with a revolver on his hip, he proudly exhibited the bullet holes in his hat. "Got 'em in my trousers, too," he told the startled Galilee. "But they weren't on me at the time. Fortunately the enemy doesn't aim so straight when we're wearing our clothes."

Then Mickey got down to business. First, he was much disturbed by the high percentage of head wounds in the Negev. Partly, he conceded, it was because curious Palmach youngsters insisted on poking their heads up above trenches to look at approaching tanks; but proper field helmets would make a big difference.

Next, he wanted more military boots. And finally, of course, there was the ever-present problem of arms. "You've got a good army down in the desert. With the right weapons, they could be the best in the world. I hear you've received some new Swiss guns. For Heaven's sake, get them onto half-tracks and move them down there, fast."

A decisive battle was shaping up in the Negev. The main Egyptian column, although slowed both by Carmi's reckless night raiders and the heroic resistance of coastal settlements, had managed to batter its way northward to the outskirts of Ashdod, only twenty miles below Tel-Aviv.

Facing the Egyptians was the Givati Brigade, holding a long, straggly line of seventeen positions and severely weakened by its April losses on the central front. A handful of Palmach's "Wild Beast" desert rovers was being rushed to Givati's assistance.

The Egyptian armor was in excellent position for a breakthrough at Ashdod. The invaders had both superior strength and the tactical initiative. They could choose their points of attack. But the commander of the column, Mohammed Neguib, was not sure how much opposition he would meet. He had been stung by the quick-slashing raiders, and astonished by the furious refusal of the settlers to be overrun. The verve that had marked his initial dash across the frontier was gone; doubt and caution, those military plagues that Mickey had been determined to transfer to the enemy, were beginning to creep in.

Neguib hesitated, long enough for the 20 mm. guns and half-tracks requested by Mickey to be shipped south; long enough for Dov Avidan, the Givati commander, to launch a daring attack against one of the Egyptian flanks.

Avidan used a platoon of jeeps to bait the fast Egyptian armored cars, which came roaring forward in advance of the tank force. The armored cars, with two-pounders and machine guns blazing, chased the jeeps toward a thick orange grove where Haganah gunners were waiting with the long-barreled Swiss guns mounted on half-tracks. At five hundred yards, the converted weapons let loose, smashing the Egyptian ranks. The tanks turned tail and fled.

On the other flank, a "Wild Beast" task force charged into the Egyptian positions and set part of a vehicle compound afire before scrambling back across the lines. Simultaneously, the first Israeli-marked fighter planes appeared in the skies.

The order went out through the no-longer-jaunty Egyptian ranks: "Dig in."

Momentarily at least, the crisis in the Negev had been survived.

In the north, too, the front was being stabilized. The Palmach's gallant Moshe Dayan had checked the Syrian threat at the top of the Jordan Valley. Lower down, a brigade of Iraqis supported by Fury fighter planes had been thrown back at Gesher.

Thus, the spotlight shifted to that tortured capital which had long been at once geographically isolated from the rest of the Jewish state, and spiritually inseparable from it: Jerusalem.

It was agreed that the capital had to be held at all costs. A new brigade would be scraped up to keep its lifeline open. And Mickey Marcus would be dispatched to the central sector—to repeat, it was fervently hoped, the miracle of the Negev.

TWELVE

Jerusalem in 1948 was different in an important respect from the capital of David and Solomon. To the south and west of the original Old City, a vast new area of public buildings, commercial establishments, and residential districts had developed after World War I. The walled Old City was physically dwarfed by the New. Within Old Jerusalem's confines, however, still lay the world's greatest concentration of religious treasures, including the Church of the Holy Sepulchre, the Wailing Wall, and the fourteenth-century Mosque of Omar, built on a site associated with the Prophet Mohammed.

At the outbreak of the Arab-Israeli war, the Old City held some twenty-five hundred Jews. Mostly aged scholars, they were crowded under brutal siege into a shallow quarter along the southeast wall, sheltered from the surrounding Arabs by a force of young volunteers.

The great bulk of Jerusalem's one hundred thousand Jews lived in the New City, in a scattering of population islands crisscrossed by Arab quarters. The Jews held a cluster of districts in the north and another group in the southeast, but these were split apart by Arab enclaves in the center. Another Arab-held position—the suburb of Sheikh Jarrah to the northeast of the New City—blocked off the Hadassah Hospital and Hebrew University on Mount Scopus. Elsewhere the rival camps were mingled in a jigsaw jumble that gave neither side a decisive advantage.

All through the desperate convoy battles beginning in December of 1947, equally hard fighting had been raging against the Mufti's irregulars inside the barricade-strewn city. As Mickey had pointed out, so long as there was no continuous defense line, individual sectors and suburban settlements were in constant danger of encirclement.

On the night of May 13, the Israelis lashed out with the three-pronged "Operation Pitchfork" to tighten their lines and create an area of fire removed from population centers. In the center, they occupied the British "security zones" and dislodged Arab irregulars who had moved into Notre Dame Monastery at the junction of the Old and New Cities. Another column plunged southward through the Greek and German colonies to form a north-south defense line with previously isolated Jewish districts. And in the north, other units cleared the Sheikh Jarrah quarter, opening the road to Mount Scopus and simultaneously cutting Arab contact with Ramallah in Samaria.

The Mufti's irregulars, driven out of most of their strongholds, took refuge in the Old City—and sent frantic requests for aid to King Abdullah.

Their pleas were hardly necessary. The Transjordan ruler, determined to make an all-out bid for Jerusalem, had already decided to commit the cream of his sharply trained, preciously guarded Arab Legion.

Although supposedly in the service of Abdullah's kingdom of Transjordan, the Arab Legion was from the first financed, trained, and supplied from London. John Glubb—who soon became an Arab and a Pasha as well as a general—was the guiding genius of the Legion; and the British Brigadier Norman O. Lash was second in command.

Other British officers—nearly forty of them—were generously sprinkled through the Legion ranks. An angry diary entry of May 26 by Colonel Richard Meinertzhagen, a veteran Middle East expert of the British War Office, asserts: "There are 37 British officers serving with the Arab Legion in Palestine against the Jews and [Foreign Minister] Bevin is lying in Parliament when he says none of them are directing artillery fire against Jerusalem. I happen to know that four are doing so."

General Glubb himself is even more specific. Commenting on a May 30 order from London directing the withdrawal of all British officers temporarily allocated to the Legion, he describes this in his memoirs as a "shattering blow." He explains why: "They included all operational staff officers, both the brigade commanders and the C.O.'s of three out of the four infantry regiments, and all the trained artillery officers. The British officers were the keystone to the whole edifice in 1948."

The bulk of Glubb's legion was some six thousand frontline troops, organized mainly in four mechanized regiments comprising forty-five hundred men.

Nobody had to walk in the Arab Legion. A large fleet of modern trucks gave the infantry virtually 100 per cent motorization.

Adding punch to this mobility were fifty armored cars of South African manufacture, and a number of armored half-track carriers.

Glubb was well supplied with rifles, machine guns, three-inch mortars, and the appropriate ammunition. But his strongest department was field artillery.

Long before the declaration of hostilities, Legion troops stationed in Palestine had stuck their bayonets into the local fighting, notably in Haifa where an Arab leader credited them with inflicting "severe injury" upon the Jews.

Now the Legion swung into high gear. Beginning May 4, point-blank artillery fire was poured into the Etzioni block of settlements on the Hebron-Jerusalem road to the south— the block that Mickey had earlier wished to have evacuated. On May 11, two Legion infantry companies reinforced by armored cars and three-inch mortars overwhelmed the barbed-wire-and-mines defenses of the settlements.

To the north of Jerusalem, Legion pressure forced the abandonment of two suburbs—Atarot and Neve Yaacov— which had been blocking the Arab supply route to Ramallah.

From May 21, a synchronized pincer movement from north and south began. In the north, Legion armor combined forces with the Mufti's two thousand irregulars; in the south, regrouped Frontier Force companies joined Egyptian units of the Moslem Brotherhood in an assault upon Ramat Rachel, the southernmost Jewish suburb, a few miles above Bethlehem.

Seven times, control of the suburban height changed hands. Blasted out of their positions by day, the kibbutz-dwellers would creep up the slopes at night and wrest the settlement back from the occupiers.

It was during this savage struggle, around May 25, that Mickey Marcus first returned to the Jerusalem scene.

The critical thrust from the north against the New City came on May 23, when an Arab Legion armored column advanced along the Old City walls against the Notre Dame Monastery, just outside the Damascus and New Gates. Occupying a key position between the Arab districts in the north and the heart of Jewish Jerusalem, the monastery had been seized on May 14 by Irgun teen-agers from Arab irregulars who took possession of it as soon as the British left its doors open.

Lost in counterattack and then rewon by Palmach, the convent building now held fast under eight hours of savage attack by medium cannon, machine guns, and infantry. The decisive blow was struck by a sixteen-year-old Jewish veteran of the French underground Army, whose accurately hurled Molotov cocktail wrecked an armored car and converted it into an anti-tank obstacle.

Frustrated in the north-south pincer attempt, the Legion tried to pound Jerusalem into submission with its heavy guns. From three angles—Sheikh Jarrah, the Old City, and Egyptian-held hills in the south—shells burst indiscriminately upon public buildings, homes, and civilians in the streets. Casualties were enormous—officially estimated at five times those of London under the blitz.

The water ration in the long-besieged city went down to a glass a day. Cigarettes were valued more highly than diamonds. There was no electricity; at sundown, the city went dark.

Of all the trials to which Jerusalem was subjected, none was more cruel than the sense of helplessness against murderous artillery fire. One can almost hear the grinding of teeth behind the words of Dov Joseph, the city's wartime governor: "To have to sit helplessly while the Arabs cannonaded the city day after day and night after night . . . in the knowledge that we had no comparable cannon with which to hit back, did more to undermine public morale than almost any other hardship."

Most desperate was the plight of the Jews trapped in the Old City. Still, somehow, through siege and weariness and starvation, the Jews were hanging on, in nearly all of the New City and a fragment of the Old. More than a week after invasion, Abdullah was not much closer to being King of Jerusalem than he had been on May 15.

Undoubtedly he communicated his displeasure to his British Chief of Staff. Glubb abruptly shifted tactics.

Some eight miles west of Jerusalem, and about a mile north of the main highway, stood the twenty-nine-hundred-foot-high Radar Hill, a strong point controlling the approaches to several communities directly along the road. Among them was the Arab village of Abu Ghosh; if it could be reached by the Legion, Jerusalem would be effectively choked off.

Two Legion companies, backed by mortars and artillery, swept up from the capital in a wide arc against the single Israeli platoon holding the hilltop. After a vicious battle, the Legion succeeded in storming the position. But when they tried to extend their penetration southward to Abu Ghosh, they were stopped at the Ma'ale Hahamisha kibbutz. Repeated Arab attempts to close the ring of small encirclement failed.

From Ramallah, north of Jerusalem, Glubb now brought down his entire Fourth Regiment and his strategic reserve of heavy artillery to garrison the key bastion of Latrun. His plan was simple: by clamping the Jerusalem supply road permanently shut at Latrun, he would bring the stubborn defenders of Jerusalem to their knees.

Latrun was not a single town, but a network of bristling defenses running east and west along a series of roller-coaster ridges averaging a thousand feet in height. It was possibly the most impregnable position in all Palestine, the scene of countless historic battles.

To the natural advantages of Latrun's rugged terrain, the British Army had added the skills of its best military engineers. A huge police station, thick-walled and skillfully designed, crowned the westernmost ridge. At the opposite end of the system, on a thirteen-hundred-foot crest commanding a sweeping view of the entire area, the main artillery post was set up. Trenches were dug into the adjoining slopes, and strong points in the nearby Arab villages gave depth to the defense complex.

Added to this, between the police station and the artillery

crest of Gun Hill stood an imposing stone monastery about the size of New York's Metropolitan Museum. The Legion lost no time installing batteries there.

Surprisingly enough, Latrun had been briefly occupied by the Israelis during the confused early days of the invasion. Their "Operation Maccabee," after clearing the heights above Bab-el-Wad on May 15, penetrated the next night into Latrun village, which Arab irregulars had evacuated without bothering to notify the Arab Legion.

However, Yigael Yadin had barely pushed a couple of small convoys through to Jerusalem when he withdrew his occupying forces to reinforce the Egyptian front—a decision for which he was later widely criticized. The fact is that the Israeli command was then in a situation where anything it did would have been in some sense wrong; there simply were not enough troops to go around.

Now, ten days later, Latrun had emerged as the focal point of the Arab Legion drive against Jerusalem. Glubb was pouring men and arms into the compound. Somehow the Jews had to raise a force to challenge him there.

Before Mickey's return from the Negev, Ben-Gurion had ordered creation of the 7th Brigade, a new unit to be staffed by veterans of British Army service under the command of Shlomo Shamir.

Ben-Gurion, with the cries for help from Jerusalem ringing in his ears, was anxious for the new brigade to go into action against Latrun at once. Shamir protested that an organization of such size—not to say an attack plan—could not be created in the few days allotted to him. He pointed to the multiplicity of languages among his troops—no less than eight; the fact that he was short of uniforms, rifles, and water bottles; and the desirability for further reconnaissance.

Shamir had strong backing from Yigael Yadin, who questioned the whole idea of a direct assault upon Latrun. He felt the position could be enveloped later from the rear, and disputed Ben-Gurion's thesis that a sudden truce might find Jerusalem totally cut off.

The argument ended with Ben-Gurion agreeing to a twenty-four-hour delay; beyond that he would not budge.

Everything was ready—or as ready as fate was going to permit it to be—for "Operation Ben-Nun." The code name was a reference to Joshua, whose father's name was Nun; literally, it meant "son of Nun."

Across the silent valley, the Arab Legion waited.

The Israeli attack went badly from the first. Confused supply arrangements—about which Mickey had been warning Haganah for months—severely delayed the start of the attack. In the face of rising temperatures, the shortage of water containers was particularly severe; with only seventy army canteens on hand, beer bottles were finally strung to kits in a last-minute attempt at improvisation.

Language difficulties caused additional problems. It was nearly 4:00 A.M., instead of two, when the first trucks of the spearhead battalion pulled noisily out of camp. Soon after, the Arabs were further alerted to Israeli intentions by premature firing of the brigade's ancient 65 mm. cannon. What had been intended as a sharp night attack was fast losing any trace of surprise.

By the time both Israeli columns reached the take-off point, the sun was peering over the shoulder of the Judean hills. The largely-raw Israeli infantry, bleary-eyed and uncertain, had to form up in plain view of Legionnaires.

The Israelis moved forward—and Mickey's apprehensions were confirmed. Contrary to the Brigade's intelligence reports, Haganah faced no makeshift garrison at Latrun but the best troops of the Arab Legion, operating heavy guns and mortars whose accurate fire was directed by trained British officers. Every hillock and hollow in the terrain below the post had been carefully pinpointed according to precise firing data; now the ground was being ploughed up with devastating fire that ripped through the Israeli ranks.

Disaster mounted. From the east came the first steamy waves of a terrible *khamsin*, the airless, oven-hot desert wind.

The soldiers of the eastward-moving second Israeli column reached hurriedly for their homemade water bottles—and discovered they had spilled empty, or were broken.

Stumbling toward cover, the troops suddenly found themselves under cross fire from the supposedly harmless Arab villages of Beit Jiz and Beit Sussin, occupied the day before without Israeli knowledge by Arab Legion patrols.

Overhead, the merciless sun beat down. Haganah platoon and section officers, trying desperately to control the spreading chaos, shouted orders that were not understood. Lacking a common language with their immigrant troops, they gestured, tugged, and finally rushed forward recklessly in futile example.

The battalion suffered heavy casualties.

There was no blinking at the fact that "Ben-Nun #1" had ended in catastrophe. Perhaps, as defenders of Ben-Gurion claimed, the attack took some pressure off Jerusalem. But it was at serious cost. No less than forty wounded men had perished of thirst on the battlefield; and several of the ill-trained immigrants were found dead with the safety catch of their rifles closed.

To cap the gloomy picture, two days later an urgent radiogram arrived from Jerusalem: the Jewish garrison beyond the ancient walls was resisting no longer. The Old City, with its monuments and its memories, had passed entirely into Arab hands.

It was a grave moment, perhaps the most terrifying the young republic had yet faced.

An undeniable factor in the impasse, related both to the collapse of the Old City and the confusion at Latrun, was the fact that there was no centralized Jerusalem-front headquarters to which Haganah and Palmach alike would be answerable.

Ben-Gurion and Yadin had never been able to agree on an over-all sector commander. The rivalry between the English-schooled veterans of the Jewish Brigade and Palmach's settlement-trained guerrillas still smoldered; anyone highly praised in either camp automatically forfeited some of the admiration of the other.

The gates of defeat had not quite clanged shut; there was still the faintest of chances that the tide might be reversed. But where could the government find a knowledgeable strate-gist who enlisted the devotion of all factions—and at the same time had the dynamic personality required for leader-ship in the field?

Reduced to these terms, there was only one possible answer.

It would be an unorthodox answer, Ben Gurion readily conceded before an emergency session of his cabinet. They would be turning over what might well be the fate of Israel, and the future of untold generations, to a man with no previous record of Zionism . . . an "outsider," in fact, from America.

But had not America itself, the oldest of living democra-cies, welcomed the aid of a Lafayette, a von Steuben, a Kosciusko? And would anyone challenge the fact that Mickey Marcus had made the difference for the Israeli fighters in the Negev?

On the nineteenth of Iyar in the Hebrew year 5708—May 28, 1948 on the Christian calendar—a brief resolution was passed by the provisional government of Israel, and issued as an order under the signature of David Ben-Gurion:

"Brigadier General Stone is hereby appointed Commander of the Jerusalem Front, with command over the Etzioni, Har-El, and Seventh Brigades. General Stone is authorized to select officers and noncoms from the aforementioned three brigades to form his staff."

Up to this time, the largest body of Israeli troops under a single command had been a brigade, and there was no system of official ranks for officers. The Hebrew term used for designating Mickey's new status as head of a division was "*Aluf*"—literally "Chief," "Commander."

No Jewish soldier had held comparable rank in Palestine since the immortal Judas Maccabeus, conqueror of the Syrian tyrant Antiochus IV.

Mickey Marcus was a general in the Armies of Israel—the first in two thousand years.

THIRTEEN

At one stroke, Mickey had acquired a double accolade: the brigadier's star and the active field command repeatedly held back by the Pentagon because of his value as a planner.

But he had also inherited a huge problem that would tax to the utmost the mental, physical, and spiritual resources accumulated over a lifetime.

Mickey weighed the forces at his disposal against the well-fed, British-led Legion. He was somewhat in the situation of a Notre Dame football coach taking over the reins of a scrappy but inexperienced small-college eleven with no reserve bench; he was obliged to confine himself to tactics his men could execute. At the same time, facing a well-trained opponent massed in a goal-line stand, he could not simply ram his way through; some element of surprise was necessary.

The trick was to balance simplicity with deception—and hope for the best. No plan was foolproof; luck was a silent partner in every successful military enterprise.

As a starter, Mickey was determined to get maximum striking power from his small armored force. Chaim Laskov, leader of the armored unit, came up with an approach that Mickey found promising. Laskov would open the battle with a sharp, direct thrust at the western positions of the Latrun bastion—police station, village, and monastery; while a large infantry force circled to the rear of Gun Hill to capture the artillery post, and split apart the two Arab Legion regiments. Israeli armor and infantry would then combine to deliver the final blow. It was a bold and forceful concept requiring exact timing.

Since this would be essentially a 7th Brigade operation, Shlomo Shamir would again be in immediate command. Mickey sat down with him, Laskov, and other staff officers to work out the details, personally pursuing every step of the plan down to the company level.

The nub of Laskov's force was a score of armored cars that barely qualified for the designation, being homebuilt "sardine boxes" made up of two steel plates slapped onto a scout-car chassis. The vehicles were covered in some places only by wood and in others not at all; nonetheless, each had a turret with a traversing medium machine gun, and another fixed machine gun.

Most of the armored cars were in the first and strongest column, whose objective was the police station. Rounding out this force were five half-tracks carrying machine guns, flame throwers, and infantry; and a support company including light mortars.

Laskov's remaining two columns, assigned to the monastery and the village above it to the east, consisted of three armored cars and a platoon of infantry apiece.

The command car, flanked by two jeeps, led the way. Past scrub grass and scraggly hillocks, the procession climbed toward the take-off point, which was on high ground captured in April's "Operation Nachson." Silence enveloped the

valley, except for the infrequent bark of a far-off machine
gun.

Mickey was in splendid spirits, reacting as always with
enthusiasm to the prospects of an offensive, true to his
conviction that "an attacking army is a victorious army."

Around 2:00 A.M. on May 31, the three columns split up
to move stealthily against their individual objectives. Laskov's
armored car swung off alone onto a side road and rumbled
forward to within a couple of hundred yards of the police
station; there, a little distance down a grassy embankment,
battalion headquarters was set up. One of the accompanying
jeeps carried communications equipment; the other was for
Mickey's use.

Mickey hoisted himself out of the car and took a few deep
breaths. Normally the night air in the Jerusalem hills was
like a good Rhine wine: light and clear and dry. Tonight it
was heavy and motionless.

Mickey slapped at a fly, donned his steel helmet, and sat
down alongside Laskov under a stubby acacia tree. Although
they were within easy range of even small-arms fire, the darkness created an eerie sense of total isolation. Gradually, the
curving rim of the mountaintop came into focus, and the
bulky outcroppings of Latrun, black and ominous.

Now, a thousand feet above the valley, from the direction
of the shadowed monastery, came the first burst of fire. There
was a brief, brisk exchange—then the shooting broke off.

Laskov looked at his watch. The police station, somewhat
north and west of the monastery, would not be reached quite
as quickly as the other objectives. Nonetheless, it was just
about time for his first column to have negotiated the roundabout approach—and time for the fledgling Israeli artillery
to be opening up.

Just as the battalion commander was leaning over to check
Mickey's watch, there was the champagne-cork "plop" of a
heavy mortar firing behind them. Fifteen seconds later, a

bursting shell lighted up a corner of the vast, four-turreted police station.

The battle was on—opened with an Israeli direct hit on a Legion anti-tank gun.

Beyond the sight of the observers on the hill, Laskov's armored cars closed in rapidly. Lining up in mass formation, they poured machine-gun fire into the police station. Simultaneously, a crew of sappers blasted a gaping hole in the barbed-wire fence surrounding the station courtyard, and a dozen brave men leaped into the yard with flame throwers. Within minutes, although the Arabs fought back with six-pound anti-tank guns and small arms, the roof of the fortress was ablaze. The Israeli attack had been launched completely according to schedule.

The next phase has been recounted in the war diary of Mahmud Roussan, then a First Lieutenant and Adjutant of the Arab Legion's 4th Regiment:

Eight Jewish armored cars succeeded in penetrating the barbed wire fences surrounding the police station. We saw two open fire with a flame thrower against the windows and the large iron gate, in order to enable infantry units to enter the fortress and exterminate its defenders. . . .

Arab Legionnaires opened rapid fire from all the arms at their disposal in all directions.

The fire of the flame throwers hit two wooden constructions of the fortress and they went up in flames. Soon the entire area was bright as daylight; the enemy's night had turned into day. Thus enemy positions were easily discovered and so was the deployment of his armor.

Actually, nothing happened "easily" for either side in the hour of fighting that followed. The attackers pressed forward and Legion guns ripped back at them in all three fortified positions, lighting up the valley for miles around. The staccato crack of the high-velocity anti-tank guns became increasingly submerged in the thunder of long-range cannon.

At the hillside battalion headquarters, bullets and shrapnel thudded into the embankment. Mickey crouched intently over the radio, piecing together the reports from the commanders of the Israeli task forces. Finally the firing began to slacken off, first in the village-monastery area and then around the police station.

Mickey leaped up from the radio and cracked his fist exultantly into his palm. "Chaim, Latrun is yours!"

Field reports within a few minutes confirmed that the Israeli armor had held its gains at all points. The strong armored bridgeheads now had only to be secured by the reinforcing infantry.

Laskov radioed his reserve infantry of the 7th Brigade, posted a couple of miles from the objective, to go into action.

Seconds later, the men on the hill could hear the motors of the infantry-transport buses starting up. After a few minutes, the motor noise stopped, and an indistinct order rang out—presumably, the command to dismount from the buses. This was followed by an enormous explosion that shook the countryside.

Mickey turned to Laskov in quick alarm. "Land mines!"

Both men leaned forward to hear what would follow. There were muffled cries, apparently of distress; and then the sounds of the bus convoy in motion again. Laskov dispatched an officer to find out what had happened.

Now the radio in the signals jeep was crackling. Where were the promised infantry reinforcements?

As minutes passed, the messages grew more urgent, especially from the forces at the police station. Legion reserves had arrived; from the roof and windows of the fortress, they were showering the Israeli armored cars with grenades—a form of attack to which those of the vehicles with open tops were particularly vulnerable. The Legion six-pounders, meanwhile, had found the range and were inflicting heavy damage.

The attacking Israeli column had been intended only as a shock force to make the breakthrough, never to carry out a holding operation. Their plight was symbolized in a calm radio report to the gunners nearby in kibbutz Hulda from a young operator whose car was inside the courtyard of the police station: "Enemy has brought up twenty-five-pounders . . . Direct your shells to right. . . ." A pause. An explosion: "Our car has been set afire." Then silence.

Laskov's investigating officer returned. He had seen only the vanishing lights of the bus convoy as it withdrew toward the Israeli base camp; circumstances suggested that the first few infantrymen to alight had stepped on a pile of land mines abandoned by the roadside.

There was still a chance to salvage the situation. The blow from the Givati Battalion, descending on the Arabs from the rear, had not yet come. If it was as crisp and sudden as planned, the Legionnaires might be obliged to turn their guns around; in the ensuing confusion, the Israeli armor could regroup.

Thus far, the signals jeep had not been able to make contact with Givati.

Scanning the dimly outlined mountain spur, Mickey abruptly grabbed Laskov's arm. "Look, Chaim—beyond the monastery, to the right!"

Turning, Laskov saw a flash of fire and heard the boom of·a Legion eighteen-pounder. The source of the new fire was Imwas, one of the key positions that was to have been neutralized by the Givati flank attack.

"Where is Ammi?" shouted Mickey.

Laskov ran over to the radio jeep reiterating the importance of making contact with the Givati Battalion. But his operator was still unable to pick up any signal.

Now the Legion command, as if sensing a slip-up in the Israeli plans, opened up its guns all along the compound in a shattering display of artillery power. The scene was vividly recorded by Menahem Talmi, the Israeli infantryman-writer:

The ground seethed and fumed. It seemed to boil and boil over and explode within itself as though it were fighting with its own inner organs and heart. Machine-gun bullets by the tens of thousands were thrusting at the hills and rocks. The torn earth, which had swallowed its hail of lead a week earlier, was once again opening sudden mouths.

In the midst of this inferno, Mickey stood with Laskov under the acacia, studying the phosphorescent stream of fire streaking westward from the Legion's anti-tank guns and field cannon imbedded along the ridge. The two commanders cursed furiously and fluently—Laskov in Russian, Mickey in English.

"They're using artillery like machine guns," growled Laskov.

"It's as bad as the Normandy beaches," Mickey agreed.

"What could have happened to Ammi?"

Suddenly the American, determined to explore for himself, ducked under Laskov's restraining arm and strode into the bullet-swept darkness. Laskov promptly sent Mickey's driver after him in the jeep.

As the jeep rattled up alongside, Mickey jumped in. By now some of the Israeli attackers were falling back. It was obvious that the assault could not be sustained. Mickey and his driver circled through the rear area of the firing line, distributing water.

Even at these closer quarters, Mickey was unable to obtain any clue as to the whereabouts of the Givati Battalion. He lifted two wounded men aboard and told Gaby to start back.

As the jeep spun around, a rifle bullet pinged against its rear bumper. The vehicle had been spotted.

In an instant, machine-gun fire also was centered on the commander's car. The jeep darted sideways at a hair-raising angle, straightened up, then zigzagged through a rain of lead up the bumpy slope.

They found Laskov brooding over a disquieting piece of news. "Brigade headquarters has finally heard from Ammi.

He got stuck in Deir Ayub—reported he could not advance—and was granted permission to withdraw."

Mickey was stunned. Deir Ayub was far to the east of the crucial battle zone. The message meant that the Givati attack had been blunted, or had somehow gone wrong, almost from the start; no help could be looked for from that quarter.

Mickey was hardly listening as Laskov went on: "I'm afraid we can't possibly hold out. Once the light comes up, we'll be in danger of encirclement. I'm going to radio Shlomo: there's nothing for it but a general retreat."

Mickey waved a hand absently. "Of course." He sat down moodily in a clump of grass, toying with his revolver, the lines of weariness for the first time showing in his face.

A sullen dawn was coming up. In the east were the ghostly outlines of blood-spattered Latrun . . . still in enemy hands.

Mickey returned to the headquarters room in Hulda. There he hovered over the radio with Shlomo Shamir, seeking some hint as to the mystery of the Givati collapse. Although the Legion troops in the eastern strong points of Latrun were well entrenched and well armed, they were divided into modest groupings of company and platoon strength scattered over a considerable area. How could such forces hurl back a battalion in a local action?

"Hello, Korah one, Korah one . . ." A code message was coming in. Givati had reached its original take-off point at Bab-el-Wad and would now file a casualty report. Mickey and Shamir braced themselves and waited.

The voice came back on the air, spoke briefly, and clicked off.

The young radio operator, troubled, turned to the division commander:

"Givati lost two dead, sir."

Mickey exploded in disbelief. "What?" he roared. "That can't be right. Get a repeat on the message!"

The boy showed Mickey the number scribbled on his pad. "They said it twice, sir. There's no question about the number."

For several minutes Mickey gave vent to his indignation. The few details that could be squeezed out of Givati did little to ease his feelings.

The battalion commander had decided soon after crossing into Legion territory that he would not have time to make the deep thrust northward to Yalu that was called for in the battle plan. Instead he swung westward to the village of Deir Ayub, which he occupied without resistance; from there he set out northeastward for Gun Hill, the main objective.

Climbing the heights to the artillery post, his partly green second company ran into strong enemy fire. Two of his men fell in the first blast.

He decided the position could not be stormed without heavy casualties, so he retreated down the hill and withdrew from Deir Ayub as well, pulling back to the Israeli lines.

Laskov, steaming with anger, entered the headquarters room to file a casualty report. Mickey made no attempt to cool him down.

Later the Givati story was to emerge in clearer perspective. The officers and men of the battalion were tied by close personal bonds, all having been recruited from the same area around Tel-Aviv. Many had been friends since childhood. In an earlier engagement, the youth of an entire suburb had been wiped out; since then, for Ammi, "every death was a personal tragedy."

Furthermore, the battalion commander had been instructed by his chief, Shimon Avidan, "not to engage in any action which might result in the unnecessary loss of his men." Avidan had his "doubts about the commanders in charge of the operation, and about their plans for Latrun."

The lesson was plain. In spite of Ben-Gurion's attempt to unify his frontal command, more than a stroke of the pen was necessary to effect such a radical changeover. The habit of superindividualism—so vital to Israel's tough pioneering years—was still deeply ingrained.

Mickey could only conclude, as he told Shamir and Laskov: "There was nothing wrong with our plan. We just didn't have the people to carry it out."

In his official report to Yigael Yadin, Mickey took care not to undercut Shamir's role as field commander, saying of himself simply, "I was there, saw battle." He added: "Plan good. Artillery good. Armor excellent. Infantry disgraceful."

With the growing international sentiment in favor of a cease fire, it was necessary that Israel not be caught short when the truce bell tolled. A link, no matter how slight, had to be established between the seacoast and Jerusalem. And it had to be done fast.

Mickey, after a day of discussion with Ben-Gurion and Yadin, pondered the problem in his hotel room well into the night.

Realistically, it might not be possible to take Latrun from General Glubb. Circumstances, if not the Arab Legion, might stop him again.

And yet some lifeline, however slim, had to be laid down to the encircled capital.

Mickey went out onto his balcony, breathing deeply of the salty Mediterranean air. He looked down to the beach below, where the whitecaps surged up again and again to the darkly curving shore.

Like the sea, he would keep beating over and over at the barred gates of Latrun. But to save Jerusalem, he could no longer count on that solution alone.

FOURTEEN

The notion of piecing together a back road to Jerusalem to get around the Arab blockade had long appealed to the chiefs of Haganah, Mickey among them. Thus far, no one had succeeded in charting a path across the stony, enemy-strewn Judean wastelands. But since early in May, a series of incidents had kept alive the hopes of fashioning such a route.

A few days before the mass Arab invasion, a trio of Palmach boys stationed at Kiriat Anavim west of Jerusalem had been given emergency leave to visit Tel-Aviv, with the understanding that they would have to make their own way past the tight enemy siege. The young fighters, carrying light arms, threaded a moonlit course down the wooden slopes below the Bab-el-Wad ravine, then squirmed through gullies and slipped past Arab mountain patrols to a friendly reception at Hulda.

On May 15, a one-truck eastbound Haganah convoy, seeking to evade Latrun, was hauled and shoved onto a wadi dirt track running south of the fortress parallel to the main highway. The dirt road, protected from Arab Legion artillery posts by a ridge of hills to its north, continued through grain fields for about two miles and emerged onto the north-south Hartuv highway within a short distance from Bab-el-Wad junction. The Israelis already held the junction as well as other key heights farther east along the corridor.

A week later a lone Palmach scout, trapped by a blasted viaduct on the bullet-swept main highway below Latrun, likewise wrenched his armored car southeastward onto the same sheltered "goat path" running through the wadi. He too reached Jerusalem safely.

Still unsolved up to this point, however, was the problem of cutting a safe and consistent route between Hulda and the wadi below Latrun; haphazard successes would not be enough.

Now, for the first time, there was the faint glimmer of an answer. The clue was in the capture, just before "Ben-Nun #2," of Beit Jiz and Beit Sussin, the two Arab villages that had been so troublesome during Shamir's first attack. These small communities of one-story stone dwellings, connected by a narrow, choppy foot trail through the hills, ran due east from Hulda, extending the Israeli hand stretched toward Jerusalem by a precious four miles.

Between Beit Sussin and the Israeli positions at the Hartuv road lay a three-mile strip of no man's land. From the Arab village to the hidden wadi road below Latrun was only half that distance.

But the intervening terrain was more suitable for eagle's flight than human passage. Sprawled across the landscape was a jumble of steep, barren hills: jagged, weed-grown, split by sudden ravines and vast broken boulders . . . . No man had crossed these sun-bleached wastes for centuries.

On May 31, Mickey led a small reconnaissance party eastward from the center of Beit Sussin. With him, in a single
jeep, were Shlomo Shamir, Vivian Herzog, who was head of
Intelligence, and Amos Chorev—the Palmach scout who had
taken his armored car through the Latrun-skirting wadi.
Chorev was a round-faced, lively, hard-rubber-ball of a man
who had previously commanded Palmach forces in this area;
not even Yigael Yadin, steeped in Palestinian archaeology,
knew the terrain more intimately.

The party followed a dirt road leading out of the village
down to an ancient sandy watering-place at the foot of an
adjoining slope. Here a few date palms rounded out the biblical setting. Beyond the oasis, a rough footpath flanked by
patches of fig trees trailed off for a few hundred feet into the
hills, disappearing completely at the bottom of a bony
incline.

What was on the other side of the incline, no one could be
completely sure—but Chorev was willing to find out. Mickey
assigned two machine guns to cover him from high ground
in Beit Sussin and the Palmach scout started scrambling up
the rocky slope.

He was gone for several nerve-wracking minutes. When
he reappeared on the crest, his face was grim. Clambering
down, Chorev reported he had found a score of bodies on
the other side: Jews who had been trapped by the Arab
cross fire in the first assault on Latrun.

But he had other news: The wadi was within tempting
distance. Although the mountain barriers between were
formidably steep and treacherously pitted, he felt a course
could be plotted across them. He was willing to try to blaze
a trail by jeep.

Mickey clapped him heartily on the back. "Now you're
talking, boy!"

Shortly after sunset, Chorev piled a couple of Palmach
stalwarts into his jeep and drove to the fig patch. He pointed

the jeep up the sixty-degree incline, stepped on the gas pedal —and prayed.

Up shot the hardy little vehicle, crashing through thistle and brush, climbing the slippery surfaces of massive slabs, tumbling into muddy fissures and lurching forward out of them. Even in the dark, Chorev's uncanny memory for terrain features was a reliable guide. On reaching the initial plateau, Chorev put one of his men at the wheel and walked out in front of the jeep, surveying the way. Foot by foot, he led the jeep around yawning cleavages and over piles of tortured rock, with a hand constantly raised in quick warning or vigorous assent.

On the first downgrade, one of the Palmach boys was pitched loose. Bruised but undismayed, he returned to aid in the excruciatingly slow advance. The jeep was in constant danger of somersaulting down the mountainside; turns of the wheel had to be calculated by Chorev in inches.

But he reached bottom—then repeated the whole arduous process over two more legs of the course. On the last and worst descent, leading down to the wadi, the jeep had to be carried practically all the way.

But soon after it, and something over three hours from the time of his departure, Chorev had whisked along the dirt floor of the valley and was shaking hands with a Har-El company commander.

The news was radioed to Mickey. Quick to seize its implications, the front commander at once assigned top priority to the new venture. Chorev was asked to trace his successful course on a gigantic detail map. And the next night, as a further test, ten jeeps (including one belonging to Ben-Gurion) were rounded up, loaded with military supplies at Hulda, and sent off to trail Chorev across the mountains.

All but one got through the tortuous pass and reached Jerusalem.

It was an important breakthrough in terms of morale—

but inadequate, Mickey knew, for meeting the fundamental
problem. More than jeeploads were needed to feed and defend the capital. And it would require more than an un-
marked mountain trail to persuade U.N. truce supervisors
that the coast had been linked up with Jerusalem.

Besides, the last stretch of Chorev's route, where there was
an abrupt four-hundred-foot drop to the wadi, was at the
moment untraversable by any vehicle; the whole convoy, like
the pioneer car of the night before, had had to be nursed
down the slope by hand.

Mickey summoned Shamir, Laskov, and a few others to
hasty conference. For more than an hour he listened to the
arguments of his most valued young aides—and finally to an
intuition developed over three decades of leadership and
planning.

To win a decision at Jerusalem, Mickey concluded, he
would have to make one . . . commit himself and his forces
in one of those calculated gambles that explode—and sometimes fizzle—across the pages of military history. The movement of emergency supplies over the hills would be continued
—by jeep, muscle, and any other means available. But simultaneously work must be started on a true road, wide enough
to accommodate trucks, and ending in a serpentine section
that would wind down the last stretch of sheer cliff overlook-
ing the wadi.

It would be a desperately difficult undertaking. Failure
would be an appalling blow to Jewish hopes; probably the
final one. To a subordinate who offered this somber reminder,
Mickey made a reply in which the jest typically camouflaged
the determination beneath: "We made it across the Red
Sea, didn't we?"

The second and permanent "Burma Road" would start,
Mickey ruled, at right angles from the original one. Chorev's
trail ran northward from the big grove at Beit Sussin, then
shifted east; the full-scale truck route would, in the interests

of saving time, head directly eastward, slicing across the mountaintops with a minimum of zigzags.

The plan ran into immediate opposition. The Chief Engineer of the 7th Brigade, reconnoitering the proposed route with Mickey, Shamir, and Vivian Herzog, shook his head. The grade was too steep; no proper grip could be dug into such hills.

Mickey faced the engineer squarely. "I don't think you understand. We're not discussing whether to build a road —but how!"

"But there are physical limits. I tell you, it's impossible!"

"Back in the fourteenth century," the American replied, "Spanish troops carved two hundred steps up a cliff in Corsica during a single night. That must have seemed impossible to somebody at the time, too!"

The engineer threw up his hands.

Here Shlomo Shamir, who had a formiable technical background, made a major contribution. Hauling the protesting engineer once more up the ragged incline, Shamir laid out with stone markers a projected path which, the engineer finally conceded, might just barely prove workable.

"Barely is all I ask!" Mickey beamed. He got off an urgent radio message to Ben-Gurion: "Can build road if you give me the equipment. Need bulldozers, compressors, stonecutters and builders—but top priority for bulldozers." Soldiers, Mickey felt, could start leveling out the relatively traversable segment of road between Hulda and Beit Sussin; but nothing less than bulldozers could begin to smash a path through the naked limestone hills.

Mickey followed up his message with a flying visit to Ben-Gurion. This was an opportunity to be grasped at once, he told Ben-Gurion; it could make a life-or-death difference to Jerusalem.

Yigael Yadin agreed. Within minutes, the matter was settled.

A bulldozer was commandeered and sent rumbling eastward. From Tel-Aviv, Jerusalem, and Ramat Rachel, grizzled stonecutters and laborers came swarming into the area to report to the Jerusalem Front commander.

Mickey had no illusions about the difficulty of his task. With one eye on the Arab Legion at Latrun, which could be kept off balance only by persistent hammering, he had to organize a military-civilian operation of enormous complexity and eggshell delicacy. The secret road he was carving, across terrain that would have given pause to a mountain lion, would have to be built literally under the noses of the enemy.

There were Arabs to his left at Latrun, in some sectors less than five hundred yards away; and Arabs on his right around Hartuv, where irregulars were operating under Egyptian command. Enemy patrols were constantly poking at the Israeli positions; if any should slip through and discover what was going on, the "Burma Road" would be destroyed by Legion artillery in a matter of hours.

To make detection more difficult, work would have to be done mainly at night. Before it could get properly under way, strong points lining the narrow corridor would have to be occupied and kept under constant guard. Other troops would keep moving along the hills in small units, providing a mobile protective screen for the unarmed roadworkers.

This operation was assigned, along the western part of the trail, to infantrymen of the 7th Brigade. East of Beit Sussin, Mickey gave Palmach troops from Har-El the task of manning high-ground outposts and keeping the nearby hills clear of Arab observers.

Now the first bulldozer arrived, and was taken over with whoops of enthusiasm by Shamir's engineers. Like a vast yellow rhinoceros, the caterpillar tractor lunged across the ground of the eastern hills, flattening folds and ridges, slamming through thick-walled terraces to clog the air with clouds of reddish dust.

Meanwhile, the emergency transfusion for Jerusalem along Chorev's temporary "Palmach Road" was already under way, via as picturesque a caravan as ever graced the biblical trade routes of King Solomon. From Hulda, where four hundred tons of supplies had been assembled, there crawled eastward a nightly procession of donkeys, camels, mules, oxcarts, and jeeps, loaded with flour sacks, canned goods and arms.

Over the bumpy knolls the convoys stumbled in thin moonlight to the first village, Beit Jiz. Between Beit Jiz and Beit Sussin passed hundreds of laborers who were filling mud holes, dragging away stones, and widening the path for the larger vehicles soon to come.

At the watering place outside Beit Sussin, animals and jeeps began the dangerous climb along Chorev's trail, guided through the darkness by half-naked sentries. Each convoy finally drew up and unloaded on the steep height above the wadi, as yet impassable.

Now the task was taken up by the Jerusalem contingent . . . veteran pioneers from the capital's Home Guard, waiting in the dry riverbed below. One by one they fought their way up the steep slope, hanging on to tree stumps and crevices.

At the top, they hoisted onto their shoulders the mule-drawn cargo from Hulda and staggered down the incline again, each man clinging to the shirttail of the one in front of him . . . a human chain of volunteers. Most were past fifty. Yet, according to Dov Joseph, then military governor of Jerusalem, "for five nights, every one of two hundred men carried a forty-five pound sack of flour over the three-mile stretch to the Jerusalem road . . . two trips a night."

Between Beit Sussin and the wadi, the nighttime hills resounded with the clatter of the bulldozer crew. Working with concentrated fury, and aided by scores of experienced quarriers from Jerusalem, Shamir's men had now succeeded in blasting out a considerable stretch of primitive but service-able mountain road. The big remaining obstacle was the near-perpendicular drop from the hillcrest loading point to the floor of the wadi below.

Here, even before the tricky serpentine passage could be completed, the engineers laid down a water pipeline. Thousands of gallons of the precious fluid, from cisterns filled at Hulda, flowed downhill into the long-empty tanks of trucks from thirsty Jerusalem.

Now a second bulldozer was brought up. Wire netting was spread over the rocky roadbed, and trampled down by the giant tractors.

Finally, after five days, a lone jeep driver, a handkerchief over his nose to keep out the swirling dust, made the perilous descent over the serpentine. He was followed by a daredevil in a taxi who all but plunged over the cliff, but made a two-wheeled recovery to reach the valley floor alive.

True, both vehicles had to be hauled back up the hill by the second bulldozer; but the "impossible" slope had been all but subdued, and a milestone reached in the epic drama of Israel's "Burma Road."

It was a drama played often in whispers, mostly in darkness, against crackling enemy fire.

The Arab Legion was first alerted when villagers in the Latrun area reported an influx of Israeli civilians. Then came the din of construction machines, and a column of dust rising from shattered rock. By the third night, it was obvious that something was up. The batteries on Gun Hill started barking.

Howitzer and mortar shells streaked across the valleys to rain down among the unarmed roadworkers.

Mickey, realizing the strain on his overage builders and porters, circulated among them, slapping backs and spinning tall stories. His presence, as ever, had a heartening effect.

After forty-eight hours, the artillery pressure abated.

More tense and continuous was the duel of ground patrols.

From north and south, under cover of night, small groups of Arabs probed at the slender Israeli corridor, seeking to slip through woods and wadis to find out what lay behind the Haganah defenses. It was against this that the American commander, working in close collaboration with Shamir and Laskov, had laid his plans. He knew that a single gap in the Israeli screen, once exploited by enemy scouts, would invite a massive artillery assault destroying road and builders alike.

The Israeli counterforces, split up into sections of six to nine men, were assigned either to ambush-posts or mobile patrols. The ambush units were stationed at all major approach points to the rolling hills, with terse orders: "Shoot at anything that appears on the skyline." The interceptor teams prowled constantly along the corridor, alert to the slightest movement of a bush or click of a tumbling stone.

No night passed without its quota of clashes: short, sharp, and fierce. Arab losses were considerable; nor did the Israelis escape unscathed.

But the lean, fluid line held, denying the Arabs a single penetration.

Hammers clanged; engines roared; stonecutters grunted; foremen cursed. At strong points in the hills, sun-baked young riflemen crouched through the night, while behind them axes swung, donkeys brayed, and truck drivers coughed in the thick dust.

Towering over the entire turbulent scene was the sturdy figure of the brigadier from America: organizing, coaxing, shaping the path hewn through rock and shellfire that was to be popularly hailed as the "Marcus Road."

Mickey was everywhere: supervising convoys, checking schedules with engineers, inspecting the ammunition issued to patrols. Day and night his jeep bounced along the route, pausing while the front commander leaped out to drop a word of friendship or advice.

Many men, including Shamir himself, were instrumental

in building the Marcus Road; but Mickey was the magnetic rallying-point. He was in his own person a kind of Burma Road for the embattled Israelis: a link to the world of normalcy and good cheer, to the future and to hope . . . a single strand of apparently indestructible humanity.

Mickey stretched out on his cot at Hulda, hands clasped behind his head. It was imperative to strike again at Latrun: hopefully, to drive the Legion out; minimally, to keep them so occupied they would not interfere with the building of the road or embark on other adventures.

For the third assault on Latrun, Yigael Alon's Yiftach Brigade of Palmach was brought down from the Galilee and placed under the Jerusalem Front command, reinforcing the battered battalions of the 7th, Etzioni, and Palmach Har-El Brigades. The new plan—dubbed "Operation Yoram" after one of King David's army commanders—was worked out by Mickey and Yitzchak Rabin, the Palmach Chief of Operations.

On June 7, a week from the time of its inception, the Marcus Road was to be completed for the Tel-Aviv-Jerusalem passage of large vehicles.

The third attack on Latrun could not be postponed any longer, if only to ensure safe passage of the massive shipments that would now be going through to Jerusalem. Matters were also coming to a head on the truce talks: Count Folke Bernadotte, the U.N. mediator, had just fixed the cease-fire date at four days away. Within these few days the fate of Jerusalem would be decided. Ben-Gurion was extremely anxious for action.

On the evening of June 8, Mickey sped eastward with an aide over the now-functioning Marcus Road toward Abu Ghosh, the ancient mountain village a few miles west of Jerusalem near which Palmach had its central front headquarters.

As they traveled, a hail of sniper fire came from the surrounding hills.

The aide spun his wheels around, stepped on the gas, and headed for the tree-sheltered sidelines. The jeep darted through the gauntlet with no worse damage than a bullet-crumpled fender.

The purpose of the trip was to confer with Yigael Alon. The earnest and gifted young Palmach chieftain, whose shock troops had absorbed fearful punishment in carrying the main burden of the six-month struggle, had been plainly hesitant about charging into "Yoram." He felt his men needed a rest; and it was also clear that he had reservations about repeating the attempt against heavily held Latrun.

Mickey sat with Yigael Alon astride a stone fence that marked the perimeter of the camp. He spoke kindly but candidly.

"I know your boys are tired. Yigael; but so are the enemy. One good punch now may make the difference.

"It's simply not your business to choose between Latrun and Ramallah. That's a policy decision, and it's been made by the heads of government in Tel-Aviv. You're a soldier; your job is to fight."

Four hours later, the first needle-jabs of "Yoram" were under way. The attack got off to a blazing start. The diversity and timing of the Israeli blows created the anticipated confusion among the defenders, leading to abrupt troop movements followed by hasty reversals.

The pay-off operation was to be initiated at 2:00 A.M. by Har-El's 5th Battalion, departing from Outpost Number 7 South of the objective. Har-El was to drive against the Arab Legion's position Number 13 on Yalu Ridge, in the center of the long, fortified enemy line.

After the one-thousand-foot hill had been seized, Yiftach's Third Battalion was to come up from Israeli Outpost Number 22 farther east, march through the captured position, and deliver the crusher against Gun Hill.

The terrain had been carefully charted the night before by Palmach patrols. The key landmark for the Har-El takeoff northward was a lone cypress on the edge of a shallow wadi.

Unhappily, a second wadi slanted off to the northwest a few yards away from the first one. The new moon had not yet come up. In the murky light, the young officer leading the first Har-El column took his men along the left-hand, more westerly path.

As a result, when the Har-El battalion completed its climb, it faced not Position Number 13, as planned, but Legion Outpost Number 14, farther west. However, the Israeli battalion did not know where it was. It attacked on schedule, and in a stubborn two-hour engagement secured a foothold . . . on the wrong position.

In due course the Yiftach forces approached Position Number 13 from a more easterly route. The post was silent; presumably it had fallen into Har-El's hands. Marching confidently in close formation, Yiftach suddenly ran into a withering blast of machine-gun fire and hand grenades at twenty-yard range. Badly cut up, the battalion fell back.

At dawn, Mickey found himself with one battalion isolated on an enemy-flanked hilltop, and the other precariously scattered in no man's land. As he radioed Yadin, "Of course I was compelled to withdraw both."

Once again, Latrun had not been overcome. Messages of self-congratulation flew through the Arab camp.

But the Legion was celebrating an empty victory. Even as shellfire and rockets tore apart the skies above Yalu, over the round-humped hills to the south a sixty-five-ton convoy was thundering across the Marcus Road to Jerusalem. Legion commanders were still taking bows as Israeli trucks poured into the ecstatic capital, bringing flour, fresh oranges, milk powder, fuel, and ammunition.

One night later, the load along the new route was more than doubled. The siege of Jerusalem had been lifted.

The modest officer-in-command made no bid for laurels, but recognition of his pivotal role was unanimous. In the *New Palestine* and the *Hadassah Newsletter*, credit for hammering out the secret lifeline was awarded to "the American hero, Brigadier Marcus." Private letters from Jerusalem referred repeatedly and joyously to "our life-saving Marcus Road"; and an Israeli monument commemorating the route acknowledges formally the overriding responsibility of "our commander Mickey Marcus who came to us from afar, a fighting man who knew the souls of men."

FIFTEEN

Older than the Bible, the village of Abu Ghosh ambles along a gentle slope some eight miles west of Jerusalem. Lush groves of plum and orange cover the hillside. The white houses and venerable terraces of the village look out over a magnificent panorama of vineyards, valleys, and mountains.

It was here that Mickey returned after "Operation Yoram" to plan his next move.

The truce had been "definitely" fixed for 10:00 A.M. Israeli time on June 11—now only twenty-four hours away. However, no one could be sure that the Arabs would obey it. And in any case, Mickey was certain that the enemy would make a last-minute attempt to improve their positions.

So long as the fighting continued, there was the danger that the "Burma Road" would be discovered—by accident, if not by design. If the road should be cut just before the cease-fire, the truce teams would declare Jerusalem an isolated position, ineligible for supplies. Condemned to a new round of starvation and frustration, the capital might well go under.

He abruptly ordered the Etzioni Brigade:

In light of present cease-fire order and the active movements of the enemy, which threaten your front, please take all steps and measures to safeguard all positions. Alert your command and advise them that the enemy may make bold and aggressive moves tonight. Consider this mission of highest priority, and you will abandon all plans to assist in Latrun attack.

Similar orders went out to all units in the divisional command. Guard posts were to be strengthened, and extraordinary watches maintained at every local headquarters. The Arabs were on the prowl.

Palmach had a surprise for Mickey. To celebrate the imminent truce, an evening *kumsitz* would be staged in the grand tradition.

An exotic assortment of delicacies had been rounded up, such as had passed no soldier's lips for months. Mickey, squatting cross-legged on the cool grass with the senior chiefs of Palmach, found himself confronting heaps of black caviar foraged from the kitchen of Jerusalem's King David Hotel; a roasted lamb; mounds of fresh plums, pears, and oranges; and quantities of wine and brandy. For men whose recent dinners had consisted mainly of thin onion soup, this was a royal feast.

Nonetheless, the American commander was at first still engrossed in the problems of war.

The truce would have to be utilized, he declared, not only for rest but for rebuilding units. Lack of training had caused many casualties: "Now we will intensify instruction and save lives."

Mickey noticed that he was being regarded with bafflement, not to say dismay. The whole point of the party, after all, had been to make him forget the war.

He poured himself a glass of brandy. Holding it up, he offered a toast: "Comrades-in-arms, *le chaim* (to life)!"

Now Mickey plunged into the festivities with his old gaiety, leading the way in several hours of uninterrupted good cheer. No one quipped with greater exuberance; no one joined more lustily in the Army songs; and no one did so handsomely by the food.

It was well after midnight before the last plates had been scraped clean and the last choruses died away. A slender crescent of new moon had peered out briefly between grayish clouds, then disappeared. The celebrants rolled to their feet, patting their stomachs in fond recollection of the banquet.

Mickey lay half-dressed on his cot, a cooling breeze lapping at his bare legs. Normally, he dropped off the moment his head touched the pillow. But tonight he was too stimulated—not only by the camaraderie of the evening, but by the climactic quality of the wartime moment.

The terrible opening round was over, and the Israelis had survived. Never again would the pressure be so overwhelming.

On every front, the Israelis had averted disaster by a hair, "winning the close ones" time and again by coming through with a last extra ounce of determination. Forced to shift their troops constantly under the weight of a five-pronged invasion, they had nonetheless managed to keep attacking. Unblessed with reserves in the usual military sense, they possessed infinite reserves in the courage of each Israeli fighter, as if the accumulated will-to-liberty bottled up over the centuries had suddenly and irresistibly been released.

In all Israel, the tank-led intruders had taken only a half-dozen points, and no decisive ones. The Old City had fallen, along with a pair of Jerusalem suburbs, two Negev settlements, and a farming village in the eastern Galilee.

All the rest of the Galilee was in Israeli hands, including the western sector originally allocated to the Arabs. In the center, the Jews had a firm grip on the New City and a freshly built highway linking it to the coast. And in the south the Egyptian Army, stringing an east-west defense line across the Negev, would soon be as much threatened as threatening.

And along all the borders so recently crossed by the invaders, Arab refugees were streaming out of Israel, the helpless victims, in the surprising words of General Glubb, of the "utterly disastrous" goading of politicians, who "encouraged them to be defiant" rather than to accept the "many opportunities for compromise offered them."

In the fires of the month just past, not only a new state had been forged, but an army capable of defending it. Yadin, Laskov, Shamir, Alon, Dayan—these were fine men and fine officers. They had absorbed with incredible speed the essentials of military organization, planning, and operations. And the troops of Israel had displayed bravery beyond expectation; buttressed by proper training, they would be a match for any army in the world.

As for himself, Mickey had done the job he set out to do. Israel was now a fact of history. In Nazi Germany, to be a Jew had been a crime punishable by death. Here, in the fighting Jewish republic, it was a mark of dignity and valor.

At long last, and with a clear conscience, he could go back to Emma.

Mickey sighed and looked at the radium-bright hands of his wrist watch. Two-fifteen A.M. In Flatbush, that would be eight-fifteen in the evening. His "Snippy" would be in the kitchen, finishing up the dishes. He could see the curve of her cheek as she reached out for a towel, and hear the tinkling warmth of her laughter.

His body was restless, and his nerves on edge. Outside the window, the branches of a tall cypress rustled with a kind of low keening. The wind from the west—the wind of freedom—was strong. He peered into the night. The sky, usually alive with stars, was blanketed by low mist; the moon was long since gone.

Mickey spun up from the cot. He shivered in his light

khaki shorts. Pulling the sheet from the bed, he threw it around his shoulders, slipped into his sandals, and padded quietly downstairs.

Outside in the courtyard, he felt the special hush that pervades a place where many persons are asleep. The crunch of pebbles under his feet was like crackling thunder.

As he crossed the clearing toward the fence, a guard stepped out of the shadows. Ordinarily, the password in danger zones was an exchange of dialogue in which some code phrase would be spelled out alternately by the two parties. In this case, however, the sentry recognized his front commander, waved a battle-weary hand, and returned to his post.

Mickey waved back, stepped across the fence, and was swallowed up in the darkness of the ridge. The time was 3:35 A.M.

Shortly afterward, the guard was pleasantly surprised to see his relief man, a recruit from Eastern Europe, emerge in battle dress from a tent. Technically, their changeover was not due until 4:00 A.M.; each man was assigned to a four-hour tour of duty. But the Har-El veteran on the midnight shift, sleep-starved from months of fighting, was glad enough to yawn his way to an early repose.

The relief man had come on early out of a deep sense of duty. Although in the country only a few weeks, and reared in an Orthodox tradition that abhorred violence, he had already had a taste of combat against the Arab Legion in Jerusalem, and took pride in showing he could meet the demands of his new country. He slung his rifle over his shoulder and began walking his patrol.

Within minutes, he heard trampling sounds in the brush to the north. Remembering his orders to keep a special alert, he tensed and brought his rifle to the ready.

At first, he could make out nothing in the blackness. Then, he glimpsed something moving—a dim figure in white.

"*Mi sham?*" ("Who goes there?"), he called out sharply.

An indistinct answer, muted by the wind, floated back.

Was it in English, that phrase coming out of the woods—
or Hebrew spoken in the accents of English? He could not
be sure, since he was not adept in either language. But he had
heard the talk of the Legion's British commanders in Jerusalem, and he knew they were encamped before Ma'ale Hahamisha, a scant valley away.

His brief emergency training had not equipped him to deal
with such a situation. Yet his responsibility, he felt, was
heavy: a major headquarters was at his back.

The guard stiffened, swallowed, and fired a warning shot
in the air.

Still talking, the white-garbed figure kept advancing toward
him, leaping nimbly over the stone fence. One hand was
flung upward: in friendly salutation, or was it to hurl a
grenade?

In the shadowed gloom, the young sentry could not tell.
His imagination told him that another second might be too
late. Trembling, he lowered his rifle. Faithful to the daily
drills he had been absorbing, he tightened his finger on the
trigger . . . and squeezed.

It was a combination of circumstances that would not be
repeated in a hundred years: the moonless, mist-shrouded
night; the early change of guards; the confusion of accents;
and the single inexpert shot that sped unerringly into the
darkness.

Mickey lay lifeless in front of the low stone wall, a bullet
through his heart. He was wearing the shorts cut for him by
the Egyptian Spitfire in the Negev.

Mickey was struck down within a hundred feet of the spot
where, two thousand years before, the immortal warrior-
king David, for whom he was named, had danced and sung
in praise of the Lord. He fell at 3:50 A.M., six hours and
ten minutes before the guns went silent . . . the last casualty
before the truce on the Israeli side.

In the morning hush, the leaders of the Jewish state sat

like gray grieving statues while David Ben-Gurion read aloud his cable assuring Emma Marcus that her husband's military gifts and qualities of character had won him "an undying place of honor in our history":

"As Supreme Commander on the Jerusalem Front, he became immediately the moving spirit of that campaign, the most difficult and far-reachingly important one we have had to fight so far."

To a newspaper interviewer, the Prime Minister put it more simply: "He was the best man we had."

The citizen-soldiers of Israel were stunned as they had not been by five Arab armies. Soon they were to demonstrate, in a series of dazzling offensives, how well they had mastered the "striking fist" designed by their brigadier from Brooklyn; but for the moment they were drenched in a flood of emotion poignantly captured in a letter to Emma from Eve Kirshner, the Tel-Aviv housewife at whose home Mickey had once briefly stayed:

"It is not only in my name that I write to you, but also a little bit in the name of the thousands of girls and boys of the Palmach, who will never dare write you and who loved your husband as well as he deserved and as much as he never could have guessed.

"From the very few words he told me, from your picture in his room, I could guess how dearly he loved you and how much you meant to him. Speaking to you is another way of speaking to him.

"We all knew him but a short time. But he belonged to those rare people whose purity brings out the best in others from the first minute. He arrived here under the name of Stone. He left us as Mickey and "Habub," an endearing name our soldiers gave him, which means "darling" in Arabic.

"I want you to know that when his men learned that Mickey was killed, they wept. Those boys, most of whom are but children, do not cry easily and death is a common, accepted thing with them . . . but this time they were not ashamed to cry.

"The day of his death will remain for us a day of mourning for as long as we live, and our children and grandchildren will be taught to love and admire the American soldier who came to our help in this desperate, difficult fight.

"Many could come, but he was the only one who came; and we will never forget it."

EPILOGUE

Under a bright and deep blue sky, they brought Mickey Marcus back to West Point.

His body had been flown to the United States by special military transport on June 30, fulfilling to the letter his pledge to be "home by the end of June." In the few days since his death, the tears and tributes had flowed from every corner of the world. The Palestinian struggle, editorialized the New York Herald Tribune, would henceforth be seen in a new light "because a good American came to it by a route that thousands of his countrymen followed a part of the way, over the beaches in Normandy . . . to the shame and shock of Dachau."

Mickey's last trip began from Union Temple in Brooklyn. Past thickly-lined streets, the sixty-car cortege wound its way to New York City Hall, where a shirt-sleeved throng of nearly two thousand overflowed police lines to join Mayor William

184 · CAST A GIANT SHADOW

O'Dwyer and representatives of the city departments in a bareheaded, silent four-minute tribute.

Then the black limousines rolled solemnly up the east bank of the Hudson.

Across Bear Mountain bridge, at the Old Cadet Chapel in the cemetery below Storm King Mountain, Governor Thomas E. Dewey was waiting, with General Maxwell D. Taylor, then Superintendent of the Academy, and Henry Morgenthau, Jr., Roosevelt's wartime Secretary of the Treasury.

It was a day of sun-washed serenity. A light breeze ruffled the Hudson; the earth, bursting with flower buds, smelled of newness and hope. In the upward-twisting branches of the great elms and horse chestnuts, robins and Canadian warblers created a light symphony overhead.

Benumbed, Emma Marcus moved forward, dimly conscious of silent, sorrowing faces and a blur of mingled sounds: the muffled Army band . . . the slow, reluctant shuffle of feet over the warm earth . . . the piercing cry of a solitary blue jay.

Surrounded by friends, she had never felt so alone, nor so baffled by the mystery of Mickey Marcus and the inconceivable accident that had cut short his vivid career. Mickey, the vital and strong—in the very flowering, as General Clay had told her, of his true greatness—would be with her no more.

The color guard came to a halt, and the bird choir fell quiet. Across the grave, the six honorary pallbearers from Mickey's Class of 1924 faced his family. Alongside Big Mike were two of Israel's toughest fighters, Moshe Dayan of the famous eyepatch, and Yosef Hamburger, Haganah commander aboard the original S. S. Exodus.

The Stars and Stripes were lifted from the coffin, and Rabbi Sidney Tedesche scattered carnations over the bare pine box. The twelve-man firing squad raised their rifles. Three sharp volleys rang out, echoing back desolately from the cliffs across the Hudson.

A young bugler stepped forward to sound taps.

As the slow, heartbreaking tones swelled out across the river, clean and pure and true, suddenly the exquisite rightness of the setting and the wholeness of Mickey's short life broke through to Emma. Mickey had fought one long battle for principles as sacred to the Founding Fathers as to the Prophets of Israel.

Emma's head came up proudly. So long as democracy lived, her husband would not be forgotten. The battered refugees and bright-eyed children of a new nation would always hear his quick, sure footsteps guarding the Judean hills. And in the halls of West Point, no final taps would ever sound for the courage and integrity and simple humanity that were Mickey Marcus.

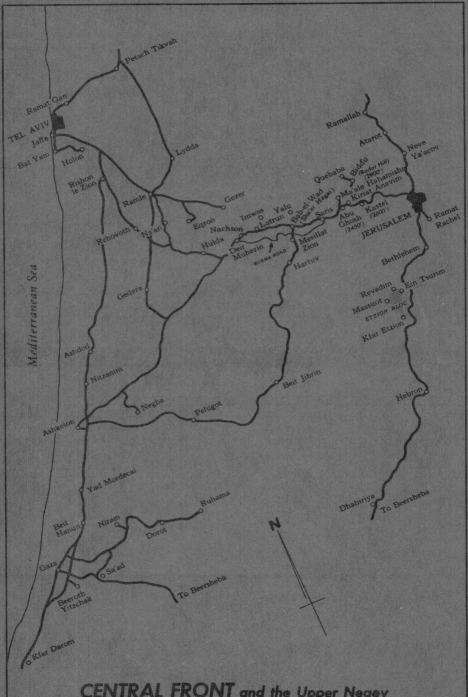

CENTRAL FRONT and the Upper Negev